IS THIS FOR A GRADE?

A Survival Guide for Teaching in the '90s

IS THIS FOR A GRADE?
A Survival Guide for Teaching in the '90s

by

Dallin Malmgren

Corona Publishing Company
San Antonio, Texas
1994

For Information:
Corona Publishing Company
P. O. Drawer 12407
San Antonio, Texas 78212

Library of Congress Catalog Card Number 94-70041
ISBN 0-931722-98-5

Manufactured in the United States of America

To Carl and Ascia,
who taught me the value of a good education.

CONTENTS

PREFACE
My education—a personal history

If you had told me back when I was in high school that I would end up as an English teacher, I might have laughed in your face. If you had told my English teachers that . . . hoo boy, I can't imagine.

I wasn't much of a student. I don't think I made it easy on anybody who had me in a class. In fact, I'm inclined to think the hand of God has put me back in the classroom. Vengeance is mine, saith the Lord. I will repay.

I come from a family of teachers. I recently learned that my great-great-grandfather taught fourth grade in Sweden for 43 years, so I guess that set the precedent. My brother, Carl, is a professor at the University of New Orleans, and my sister Diana teaches English and Spanish at a high school in Missouri. (I have another sister, Miriam, who taught one year of elementary school in Maryland, then loaded her car and traveled across the country to find a better life. She married a millionaire from Marin County—you can tell who had the brains in the family!)

Actually, my brother had the brains. Or so it seemed to me. Every year it would be the same—on the first day of school the teacher would take roll, get to my name, struggle a bit but smile unfailingly, look up with appreciative eyes, and say, "Ah, another Malmgren." Within a month my parentage would be in question.

My brother was a tough act to follow. At honors nights he would wear out the school rug going up to the stage to collect his accolades. He wound up his high school career as a National Merit Scholar with a full ride to Stanford. I decided early on there was no percentage in following in his footsteps—he had the whole pavement covered. I sought other forms of recognition: I clowned around. Unfortunately, my parents put the highest possible premium on academic success. So goes the story of Golden Boy and Black Sheep.

I have another explanation for my educational difficulties. I never went to kindergarten, so I didn't get a chance to figure out those things that Fulghum guy did. I've had to piece it together as I went along.

My elementary years were marked by difficulty and intrigue. I was intrigued by Frankie Silvestri, who could swallow a maraschino cherry whole, then bring it back up again. I had difficulty with Mrs. Gevjan in the third grade — through no fault of my own. I was in the on-deck circle during a softball game at recess. Even in the third grade I knew it was important to look cool in the on-deck circle. The dorky kids would just swing a bat as hard as they could. Not me. I took two bats and started out swinging slowly, picking up velocity as my at-bat approached. One of the bats got away from me, sailing in a perfect arc toward Mrs. Gevjan, umping at third base. Had she not raised her arms I'd have flattened her chest, a considerable achievement. I spent the next month of recesses in the principal's office.

I was intrigued by Brooke Hanlon, who invited me to kiss her after school in the fifth grade. (Not my first kiss. That was in the second grade, on a dare, with a candy bar as a reward. Poor girl never knew what hit her.) I had trouble with my mother, who viewed a death certificate as the only valid excuse for staying home from school. She didn't even buy my all-time favorite—frozen hair.

Things didn't improve much in junior high. At the beginning of eighth grade I was selected for the special "gifted" class the school was instituting. At the end of eighth grade I was summarily ejected. But I did learn humility. By junior high, girls were the rage with me. Our school had a music room, and after lunch we were allowed to go in there and dance. My heart belonged to Merle Solotoff. We made arrangements to meet at a movie on Friday night. My dad killed that plan when he learned I hadn't taken out the garbage Friday morning. All weekend I pined for Merle. On Monday I couldn't wait to get in that music room and reassure her of my devotion. Something held me up, and when I got there she was already dancing with Kenny Jones. A slow dance! Boldly I cut in. Kenny shook his head and spun away from me. I tapped his shoulder again, and he refused again. "Oh yeah," I challenged, full of myself. "Why don't we just let Merle decide?" Merle looked at me sadly. "I want to dance with him." I melted into the floor.

High school sank me deeper into the morass. In my sophomore year I made the varsity basketball team, only to have my father put me on waivers when he saw my next report card. "The grades of a truck driver," he grumbled. (And he wouldn't even teach me to drive!) I suffered the next major disaster of my life when my parents moved from Philadelphia to St. Louis between my junior and senior years. A friend advised me to just find a girl and lay low for a year. That's what I did. I don't remember learning much of anything in high school.

My college career was just as checkered. I started at the University of Missouri in September 1967 and graduated with a B.S. in Education in August 1981. Fourteen years. Remember though, I started college in the late sixties. I loved the demonstrations, I loved the sit-ins, I loved the protest marches—I didn't care much for the classrooms. I remember taking a French class; my attendance was very sporadic. The teacher used sarcasm as a cattle prod. "Ah, Monsieur Malmgren," she cooed on one of my rare appearances in class. "To what do we owe the honor of your presence in our class? Are you lost? Perhaps you are bored today? We have a test next class session. I wonder if you will come back then? I am sure your classmates hope so, for I grade on a curve." I pulled an all-nighter before her test, aced it, and never went back after that.

So how did I get educated? I'd have to credit my parents and one high school teacher. From my parents I acquired a love for reading and a respect for intelligent thought. There were always tons of books in our house. And we were inveterate library-goers.

The first library I remember sat up on a hillside, a white building with tall, dark trees surrounding it, and old-fashioned radiators under windows at the ends of long rows of books. That library still makes occasional guest appearance shots in my dreams. I don't think my dad paid too much attention to us until we were teenagers and could entertain rational thought. I still remember the thrill of saying something with a little substance at the dinner table and having him nod approvingly. Not that he courted servility. I remember one of our epic arguments. I told him I thought Adolf Hitler had some admirable leadership qualities. He couldn't handle that at all. You just couldn't talk with my father without being able to think—I liked that.

Finally, the teacher. I never had him for class, but I wish I had. I met him on a school playground; he was running a summer recreation program and I was in it. Our first link was sports. He took me to see Willie Mays play centerfield, and almost everything I know about basketball I learned from him. He taught high school English, and I suppose he's the biggest reason I ended up where I am today. He gave me Steinbeck's *In Dubious Battle,* Hemingway's *For Whom the Bell Tolls,* and Fitzgerald's *This Side of Paradise.* He wanted me to have a social conscience. He also tried to teach me self-discipline, determination, and dedication to one's goals. Years later when I realized the value of such virtues, I thought of him.

I went to see him a couple of years ago. He's still teaching high school, and he still radiates the same enthusiasm and zest for living. After thirty years! We had lunch at a restaurant in suburban Philadelphia, and ten people must have come by our table to say hello. Bob Kazanjian had an impact on my life. May I do the same for others.

IS THIS FOR A GRADE?

1
TEACHING IN THE
PUBLIC SCHOOLS
Twelve years down the road

Those who can, do.
Those who cannot, teach.
　　—George Bernard Shaw
　　(coincidentally, a high school dropout)

You can't pick up a newspaper or newsmagazine these days without reading something about the inadequate job we're doing of educating our young people in this country. Much of the blame is being placed on the teachers. Rightly so, I suppose. After all, we are the ones in the classroom with them. Teaching has become a much maligned profession, and solutions to the "education crisis" are being bandied about with the fervor of an oldtime religious revival. A teacher walks on shaky ground these days.

I have been a high school teacher for twelve years, and I am proud of it. Some of those years have been difficult, and there have been times I've come home contemplating a career change. But not too many. Those times have been far outnumbered by the "magic moments"—when I got an idea across and saw something click inside their heads, when their energy has kept me feeling young, when I knew that my being there has made a difference in someone's life. Nothing can diminish the value of those moments.

I teach English. The good thing about teaching English is that you get to talk about life. I'm weak on grammar and strong on literature and writing. (I can feel the traditionalists out there squirming already.) When we read something in my classroom, I'm far more likely to ask, "What would you have done?" or "Do you

1

think such and such made the right choice?" than I am, "What are the symbolic implications of the dying rosebush?" Real life English.

The first premise I teach in writing is that you have to find your voice. "To be a writer," I say, "you have to believe you have something to say—that what goes on inside your brain is worthy of other people's attention."

That brings me to this book. After twelve years of teaching, I have something to say. Lots of things go on inside my brain when I think about this profession, and I've developed sufficient ego to believe they are worthy of some attention. Because we need to think about what we are doing. So many negative things are being written about our educational system, and most of them by people who don't really seem to know much about it.

I am not what is called an educationist. I earned my B.S. in Ed. at the University of Missouri and got a teaching job, and the only postgrad work I've done has been to fatten up my monthly pay-check a little. I know very little about "educational theory," and I care even less. I'm completely convinced that 99% of what comes to us through our state educational agencies is fodder. You can learn more by sitting and observing on a school playground for a day than you can in a hundred university classrooms.

As for the opening quote, with all due respect for Mr. Shaw and his brilliance, I have complete disdain for his attitude. No task is more vital to the survival of a society than the education of its young people, and no one deserves more respect than the people who attempt to do it. An effective teacher must be an expert at planning, organization, improvisation, communication, and evalu-ation. He or she must also be able to play politics, manipulate recalcitrants, stretch a dollar, and invent a thirty-hour day. Put a truly great teacher into another field of endeavor, and she will zoom straight to the top. But, thank heavens, most of them prefer to teach.

So I want to write about education in the real world. The ideas for these essays were drawn from a million experiences—from heated debates in the faculty lounge, from confrontations with angry parents, from crisis interventions with distraught students, from a bad taste in my mouth after a school lunch or a meeting with an administrator, and yes, from a magic moment or two. While my experiences have come strictly at the high school level, I believe that the issues raised herein will be relevant to all teachers, and to anyone else with an honest concern for public education.

My hope for this book is that the reader who is contemplating a career in teaching will feel encouraged—encouraged to pursue with dedication and enthusiasm this trying but rewarding profession. I hope the seasoned teacher will smile in recognition, and perhaps feel stimulated to keep on keeping on. I hope those individuals who chose teaching as a *job*, who go through the motions realizing neither the privilege nor the responsibility of teaching young people, will feel the prod to get out and leave the work to the professionals. And I hope the "education critic" will walk a mile in my shoes.

I couldn't begin to thank all the people who've contributed to this book. I've known teachers who are so good they leave me awestruck. I've learned there is no "right method" for teaching; only a "right heart." Most of all, I would have to thank all those young faces who have passed through my classroom in these fast twelve years. They are the ones who make it most worthwhile.

You see, I know this much for certain—the teachers will be at the heart of any solution to the "education crisis." We care the most. After all, we are the ones in the classroom with them.

2

IT'S NOT *WHAT* YOU KNOW
The three most important people at your school

In the School of Education at the University of Missouri, I took courses like The Intellectual Foundation of Education, and Education of Exceptional Children, and Introduction to Educational Measurement and Evaluation. I don't remember a thing about any of those classes, and they have helped me not a whit in my teaching career. Further, I don't think I've ever met a teacher who felt the curriculum from any School of Education profited him or her worth a damn. Sorry, educationists.

So I've considered what I could tell a beginning teacher, one fresh out of the ivy-covered surreal world of academia and standing at the precipice overlooking the blood and concrete walls of a real classroom. Turn back! (No, just kidding.) I would say that on at least one level, the rules of business apply to the rules of education—that is, it's not what you know, it's who you know.

Pay attention, first-year teacher, and I'll tell you who you need to know. The principal's secretary. Numero Uno, the alpha and the omega, BWOC. This woman (not meant to be sexist, but it always has been for me) can make you or break you. She wields power in that most dangerous way—she knows what she can do, and you don't. But if you take the trouble to cultivate her friendship, your chances for success will improve immeasurably.

4

Realize first that this woman knows more than anyone else in the school. She knows who's leaving, who's staying, who's in trouble, who has what, who wants what, who can get what. She's like Rome—all roads lead to her. Which means that she is capable of getting things done faster than anyone. Most anything you want to do that is out of the ordinary requires a principal's signature, and she holds the key to that kingdom.

One might wonder why not just get to know the principal? Bad idea. As a matter of fact, the principal is one of the people you shouldn't get to know. There's nothing he (again, just my experience) can do for you that the secretary can't, and he usually refers you to her anyway. And principals almost always have to posture. They have to measure their responses, consider your problems in the light of the whole, and always, always evaluate the impact of what you want to do on their own job security. You are far more likely to get an honest response from the secretary.

The principal's secretary can give you job security; it's the head of housekeeping who can provide comfort. She is a valuable ally, and an enemy to be feared above all others. Every one I've ever met had a mean streak, and took a perverse pleasure in seeing how long she could string out a work order from an unfavored one. Cross this lady and your chalk disappears, your trash accumulates, your room furnishings depreciate, your thermostat malfunctions, your floor gets sticky, and your car won't start. Befriend her and you have the finest in desk chairs, classroom equipment, and janitorial services. The head of housekeeping is the mistress of the pecking order; she can dispense favors with the manipulative wiles of the cutest girl in the seventh grade. She also has as her chief ally the head of maintenance—and he can take out a whole wing of a school with the efficiency of a cruise missile.

I've discussed this topic with a number of my colleagues, and the choices for first and second most important people to know at a school were near unanimous. The third provoked a good deal more debate. My selection could be colored by my teaching field, but I choose the school librarian. At the risk of striding over cliche-ridden territory, books are the keys to knowledge, and the librarian has the keys to the books—a good person to know. On the academic plane, the librarian can help you find out something quicker than anyone. When you get one of those kids who asks a million questions, the librarian becomes a godsend.

Knowing the librarian offers other benefits besides providing a mere source of knowledge. The librarian is the only person involved in academics who controls a fluid budget. As members of the English department, we can order educational tools once a year—in February, and chances are those requests will be turned down. If there's a book or magazine you'd like to use as a reference, you need to anticipate it a year in advance. But the librarian can order materials year round, and if she is your friend and respects your motives, she is usually very accommodating. She can also become the bestower of pleasant perks. I get to see the *Sports Illustrated* swimsuit issue before she tears those pages out.

In deference to the opinions of the people I work with, I'll award a couple of honorable mentions. The registrar is a very helpful person to know. She can tell you how many people are in each class, in case you think your classes are overloaded. She can help you get the conference period you want. If you need to pull strings to get rid of a troublesome student, or change one from advanced to regular or vice versa, all those strings are attached to the registrar's office.

The accounting clerk can also be a lifesaver. She can generate cash in a matter of minutes when it might take weeks to go through the requisition/approval channels. She will also cash your personal checks if you are nice.

If all this smacks of cynicism, I apologize. I don't intend that. The real action is in the classroom, and in there you're the ringmaster. But you can run into a few roadblocks on your way to the show, and it's good to know the people who drive the bulldozers. Be kind to them.

3

TEACHING THEM TO WRITE
A voice in the wilderness

At a writers conference I attended recently, I overhead part of a conversation taking place at a table behind me. "Let's face it," a young man stated emphatically. "Most of us here became writers in spite of our teachers." That one made me squirm.

But I couldn't argue too much, because my own experience confirmed that man's opinion. I can remember the first time I ever got excited about writing something. I was in the seventh grade, and the assignment was an original story. I wrote about a guy who built a bomb shelter while all his neighbors gathered round and laughed at him. Sure enough, one day the sirens went off and the news reported that nuclear war was imminent. The neighbors rushed to the bomb shelter man and begged him for a spot in the shelter. He turned them all away. The last line of my story was, "Now where the hell did I put that key?"

Okay, it's not a great story. But I worked hard on it, and I was happy with it. When my teacher gave my story back to me, she had put a heavy red circle around the word "hell" and written beneath it, "Who do you think you are, Ernest Hemingway?" She gave me a D minus. (You can get a D minus in my class by putting your name on a paper and writing gibberish.) What a blow! It took me another fifteen years to think seriously about becoming a writer.

That's a radical example. At least, I hope it is. But something is wrong with the way we are teaching young people to write, and I think I know what it is. We seem to make a concerted effort to remove the "art" from writing, to ignore that writing is a creative activity. Witness the five-paragraph essay. I know a sophomore English teacher who boasts "If my students don't learn anything else in my class, they learn how to write the five-paragraph essay." I wonder if they learn how to escape from handcuffs?

Or what about the research paper? At my school everyone except the remedial students has to do a research paper in his sophomore, junior, and senior years. Most of the time that project takes up six weeks, or one/sixth of the school year. Research papers, especially as they are taught in high school, are the lowest form of hack writing.

This is what I tell my writers: You are pursuing an art. There are muses and obsessions and inspirations and psychic forces at work. You must be aware.

Naturally, there are plenty of reasons we've let the joy of writing slip out of our lesson plans. For one thing, we are told to. Many states now require that their high school students pass some sort of minimum skills test in order to graduate, regardless of their high school credits. This skills test contains a writing sample. These test scores show up in the local newspapers comparing neighboring school districts; therefore, they are taken very seriously by administrators. Our students spend months reviewing the criteria the evaluators use to grade the writing sample and learning to write accordingly. We don't teach them to write; we train them to pass a test.

Another reason we don't teach writing the way we should is because we have to read it. It is so much easier to grade a grammar test than a writing assignment! Especially a creative assignment, where the criteria get hazy fast. I recommend that English teachers be given one less class period a day than other teachers, with a strong admonition that they use that extra time to enhance their students' writing skills.

Happily, we can do something about our woeful record as teachers of writing without any major administrative changes. This is a problem we can solve, and the solution works on any level. I can sum it up with one basic premise: A teacher of writing who doesn't write with his students is just faking it. Learn by doing. A teacher who writes will appreciate the difficulty of each assignment and learn firsthand which ones are effective and which aren't. He will dismantle the perception of himself as an arbitrary dispenser of grades. He will enhance his own creative powers and ignite hidden powers within his students. He will descend from the podium to the porch swing. He will unleash muses and psychic forces in his classroom.

(As I write this, I'm sitting on my back porch on a Texas summer afternoon. A soft breeze is blowing, but it's hot. The cicadas are thrumming, their chorus rising and falling, creating an electric hum. My dog was lolling in the shade until she noticed a mockingbird madly chasing a squirrel through the two adjoining trees in our backyard. Now she's moving back and forth between the two trees, adding her bark to all the racket. It's like Disneyland out here. Muses are at work. Shouldn't we take our students outside to write sometimes?)

I feel very hopeful about our future writers in America. For one thing, I think there is a movement afoot within the educational community that is having a dramatic impact. Writing projects that are geared toward getting teachers to discover themselves as writers have sprung up all over the country. It started with something called the New Jersey Writing Project, I think. I attended one three summers ago, and I never saw a group of teachers so psyched up about writing and teaching as we were on the last day of the three-week seminar. Shock waves.

I can suggest some ground rules for anyone who wants to get serious about teaching writing. This always goes up on the board during the first few days in my creative writing class, and it is constantly referred to.

FIVE THINGS YOU DON'T SAY IN CREATIVE WRITING:

1) "Is this for a grade?" (They must learn to write for themselves, not for us.)

2) "How long does it have to be?" (As long as it needs to be.)

3) "I can't think of anything to write." (You're not allowed to have writer's block till you reach 40.)

4) "I wrote this but it's stupid." (Would you ask a girl, "Would you go out with me? I'm ugly.")

5) "Will you read what I just wrote, Mr. M?" (Not until you revise it, sweetie.)

Have I set myself up as an expert at the teaching of writing? That would be wrong. I do know I love seeing a student turn a phrase just right almost as much as I love turning one myself. And I don't think we teach any more important skill in a high school than the ability to write. I always tell mine that it doesn't matter what their career choice is, if they can write well they'll have a better chance for success. I also stress that writing is a form of communication. Journals and diaries are fine, but writing is like sex—it works better with two people. Writing demands an audience; just ask any writer who ever got a rejection slip. But most important, writing expresses who you are. It's like taking a snapshot of your brain.

I always tell my students that anyone who wants to be a writer has to develop a strong ego. A writer should love the sound of his own words. And, good or bad, rejection or sale, a writer has to be able to take the feedback. It's really the same for a teacher. How can you teach someone to write if you're not sure you can do it yourself? And if you write with your students, I promise you'll get feedback. Try it.

4
THE LOST R
Where have all the readers gone?

I wrote my first young adult novel, *The Whole Nine Yards,* after my second year of teaching. It is about a boy in high school who is obsessed with girls. I wanted to write something a teenage boy could relate to and would enjoy. The reason I wanted to do that was because I had observed that high school boys rarely read anything for the fun of it. Sure, you always have a few who are into science fiction or Stephen King, but, for the most part, the idea of self-motivated reading is as alien as self-motivated room cleaning. I was never one for cleaning my room, but I'd hate to think what my life would have been like without books.

I became an honest-to-God reader in the summer after fifth grade. Oh, I read before then. I can remember going through *Highlights for Children,* the Hardy Boys series, Chip Hilton, *Mad* magazine, *Marvel* comic books, etc. But on my last report card in the fifth grade, my teacher wrote, "Dallin is a very slow reader." That troubled my father. He decided I would read a book a week all summer, and write a corresponding book report! To my mind, he might just as well have stuck me in solitary confinement for three months.

But my dad had the wisdom to pick out great books. The first one was *The Earth Is the Lord's* by Taylor Caldwell. My heart sank

11

when I saw it—500 plus pages, no pictures, small print. The book jacket called it "a lusty adventure." In the fifth grade? Well, once I got going I was hooked. Staying up at night with a flashlight and everything. I felt like I had entered into a completely different world with a lot of familiar terrain. I loved it.

I became a confirmed reader, so much so that when my wife and I became engaged, I explained to her that I did have one requirement of the woman who would share my bed.

"What is it?" she asked, looking at me a little cockeyed.

"Can you sleep with the light on?" I responded.

By God's grace, Karen really wanted to marry me. "Oh yes," she assured me. "No problem. I'm out like a light as soon as my head hits the pillow."

I married her. On my next birthday I got a gift from my mother-in-law. (They work together on these things.) It was called The Itty Bitty Light, an apparatus which attaches to a book and sends a pencil beam of light onto the page being read while the rest of the room remains in complete darkness. Marriage is always about compromise.

My daughter, who just finished the eighth grade, reads compulsively. You can't keep a book out of her hands. We have to check that her light goes off late at night or she'd read until three in the morning. Start a conversation with her and you will learn in a very short time that, yes, she has read *Gone With the Wind*. Twice. My son, unfortunately, is just the opposite. I try to console myself by pretending he reads his baseball cards. When he finished the fifth grade, I tried to rectify the situation by using my father's old method. Complete failure. He looked at me like I'd lost my mind when I showed him *The Earth Is the Lord's*. The best we've done so far is a couple of Stephen King short stories.

A school librarian friend of mine thinks that apathy is too mild a word to describe the typical teenager's attitude toward books. She thinks antipathy is more accurate. To make her point she showed me some books from her library. Dark brown stains discolored the inside pages. Kids that chewed tobacco were using the books as repositories for their spit! She showed me encyclopedias and reference books with pages torn out. It saves spending a dime on the copy machine, she explained. This year the students are not allowed to bring bookbags into the library because theft has become such a problem.

What has caused our young people to hold books in such low esteem? Television has certainly been a factor. Sure, we had TV's when I was growing up, but nowadays there are VCR's, movie channels, MTV, and Arnold Schwarzenegger. Howdy Doody and Mickey Mouse were in a different ballpark.

Undeniably, the great malefactor has been that devilish machine Nintendo. In 1990 the sale of all adult trade books equaled $2.8 billion. In the same time period, Nintendo sales totaled $4.7 billion. Our children are not just playing Nintendo more often than they read; they are playing Nintendo more often than *we* read. An old friend of mine was in on the ground floor of importing Nintendo's from Japan. He owns houses on the Monterey peninsula and in Hawaii. But he carries some fierce karma. If we could magically transform all those child hours spent holding a joystick into hours spent reading books, we'd be the most literate society in the history of civilization.

Parents know this. Most every adult I talk to looks down at the floor sheepishly when he or she admits they've bought a Nintendo for their home. What price quietude?

I'd be remiss if I left all the blame resting on the parents. We teachers have part of the culpability. Similar to the way we teach writing, we seem to make a concerted effort to remove the fun from reading. Our most effective means of doing this is foisting the "classics" on them. *The Red Badge of Courage* is a fine novel, but show me a high school student who enjoys it and I'll show you a nerd. The same goes for *The Old Man and the Sea, The Great Gatsby, The Sound and the Fury, Silas Marner, The Scarlet Letter,* the works of William Shakespeare (especially *Julius Caesar* and *Hamlet*), *Crime and Punishment,* and *The Grapes of Wrath.* (All the above have been taught at my high school within the last three years.) Now, please don't misunderstand me. Three of the above would rank on my all-time top ten list, and I'm certainly not suggesting we abandon the classics in the classroom. We just have to learn to mix it up a little bit.

I have observed that many English teachers have a built-in prejudice against teaching the so-called "genre" novel (i.e., mystery, romance, science fiction, etc.). (Ironically, in terms of personal reading habits, that is what most read.) Nowhere is this bias more evident than in the young adult category. I have had two young adult novels published. I'm fairly certain that less than one-third of the English faculty at my school has read either one of them. I don't mean to be petulant, but if someone else at my school published a book, I'd want to read it.

The notion that YA books are not serious literature is horsefeathers. So much quality writing comes out of the genre. I've met many of the YA authors and have felt awed by their intensity. They are writers of serious fiction about young people. And that is the key. These books are about the people who sit in our classroom. Every year I require each of my sophomores to read a YA book. Whenever possible, I steer them toward something that might touch home. One of those "great moments in teaching" comes when a kid asks if I know of anything else he might like to read. Some of them become voracious.

In a high school year we only have them for 180 hours. That's not much time to make a mark on a young person's life, especially if you consider all the other influences coming in. The most enthusiastic, energetic teacher in the world can hardly hope to create more than a ripple. But . . . if you can turn students into readers . . . you offer them a lifetime of education . . . and your influence lasts forever . . . believe it.

In keeping with my desire to offer something of practical value within these pages, I've come up with a reading list of Young Adult novels. Any of these books could be taught on the high school or junior high level, and I promise they will hold the interest of your students more effectively than *The Red Badge of Courage*. This list could contain thousands of books — these just happen to be some of my personal favorites:

Running Loose by Chris Crutcher — a boy learns to deal with two of life's more difficult traumas, first love and death.

Tex by S. E. Hinton — surviving adolescence without parents. (You couldn't go wrong teaching any of Hinton's books.)

Abby, My Love by Hadley Irwin — a sensitive look at sexual abuse.

Killing Mr. Griffin by Lois Duncan — this one is a surefire hit with your students because Mr. Griffin is an English teacher, and they really do kill him.

Ordinary People by Judith Guest — the most insightful exploration of parent/teenager relationships that I've ever read.

The Pigman by Paul Zindel — almost a relic, but kids stil turn the pages to find out what happens to the boy and the girl and the strange man across the street.

The Chocolate War by Robert Cormier — another oldie, but if you want your class to think about peer pressure, there's nothing better.

Night Kites by M. E. Kerr — another can't-miss author, but this particular book will force your students to look at the AIDS epidemic with compassion.

Hatchet by Gary Paulsen — the best outdoor adventure writer on the YA market. Start them with this one and they'll want to read more.

Zan Hagan's Marathon by R. R. Knudson — a terrific sports book, part of a series, and guess what? Zan (Suzanne) is a girl.

Winning by Robin Brancato — another sports book (sort of), this one about a paralyzed football player.

The Ninth Issue by Dallin Malmgren — a high school newspaper staff gets radical and starts reporting what's really going on at school. (I hear the author's a nice guy.)

This is only a taste, and all of these books might not be readily available. The best way to find out what your students would like is to explore the genre yourself. Or better yet, with them.

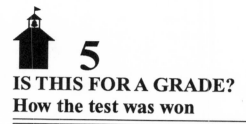

5
IS THIS FOR A GRADE?
How the test was won

Whenever I give a major test, as I am handing out the answer sheets I remind my students that in five years they will not even remember the grade they are about to make. "You just wait and see," I tell them. "When I see you in Wal-Mart five years from now, I'm going to ask you what you made on your sophomore poetry test. You won't have a clue."

I am ideologically opposed to grades. I don't believe in them. The point of a grading system is to evaluate the quality of learning taking place in your classroom (or to "measure content mastery," the educationists would say). Do my grades do that? Not ever. The problem lies with the concept. First of all, whenever making a 95 (or a 90 or 80 or 70) becomes more desirable than acquiring knowledge, the educational process has degenerated into a meaningless sham. Secondly, the higher the *quality* of learning actually taking place in a classroom becomes, the more immeasurable it is.

The only sound justification I've heard for our present system of grading is that it's an accurate reflection of how our students will be treated in the world. There's some logic in that. My annual teacher's evaluation is as big a joke as my son's report card. In fact, I've always felt that passage through the public school system is a pretty effective training ground for life in the real world, simply because of the plethora of imperfections in both.

But can you test how well a person has learned to think? I'm not sure you can even teach a person to think. Generally speaking, I feel I've had a fairly successful day in class if I'm able to frame things in such a way that my students are confronted with a situation which requires thought.

Of course, should the educationists decree we are to abandon our role as dispenser of grades, the loudest and most pained howl would arise from my fellow teachers. That's because grades are the only stick we have, and we have to have a stick to be able to beat down the dog. Picture the scene:

> **Teacher:** Now, class, get out pens and paper. I want you to write a theme on Boo Radley's role as a mockingbird.
> **Student:** Excuse me, sir, is this for a grade?
> **Teacher:** No, I want you to do it for the sake of acquiring knowledge.
> The class dissolves in raucous laughter.

So perhaps we are stuck with the system of dispensing grades, and all the incipient games it evokes. In my school district you cannot make lower than a 50% as a six weeks' average. That means if you don't do a damn thing you have made half the grade of the mythical flawless student. Knock off two 80's on the other six weeks' grades and you pass for the semester. Most of my kids can do the math behind that.

Consider also that next to standardized test scores, the failure rate is the statistic closest to an administrator's heart. A high school is, in an alarmingly accepted sense, a factory, and our end product is high school graduates. Anybody who's screwing things up on the assembly line faces the displeasure of the foreman. Most of us teachers can figure that out.

Welcome to the world of participation grades and bell curves and extra credit. I sometimes ask this question in my classroom: "Do you people believe that I, as the teacher, can manipulate my gradebook in such a way that I can give any one of you any grade I darn well feel like (above 50%) and be able to justify it within the confines of my grading system?" They humbly agree that I could, and they get back to work. Ah, power.

But I *don't* do that, and because I don't, it is inevitable that each semester, somewhere along the line, I will be faced with the ethical dilemma—Sally made a 69. She'll come to me and beg for that point. I don't blame her. One lousy point determines whether she will have to spend 90 more hours in an English classroom (probably not as interesting as mine), whether she can remain on the dance team (her top priority, no doubt), and ultimately whether or not she will graduate (mine is a required course). So do I give her the point? In my early years of teaching, the answer was an unequivocal no. It still usually is. But I'm a little more comfortable playing God now, and so I ask myself what will be of more benefit to Sally's life, to repeat the course or get the point? The answer is not always unequivocal.

The burden of stress that our grading system puts on many young people is simply inhumane. For many "honors" students, e-i-g-h-t-y-n-i-n-e spells d-i-s-a-s-t-e-r. Since one of the great onuses you can attach to a teacher is to label him "an easy grader," there exists a built-in unresolvable conflict of interests. So the kid gets to take home his disastrous report card, where it will be carefully perused by his parents. All parents of honor students are convinced that theirs are potential geniuses. (I confess that my own enlightened attitude about the meaninglessness of grades dissolves entirely when my children bring home their report cards.) Teachers perceive this stress-induced discomfort in their students with a grim satisfaction ("You made this grade the old-fashioned way—you earned it!"), but I question its educational value.

Do we trash the system? Hey, I wouldn't mind hearing: "Excuse me, sir, but is this for my educational advancement?" Music to my ears.

6

INSERVICE TRAINING
Bend over and we'll teach you to teach

Every year the teachers come back a week before the students do. I think it's our way of staking our claims on the building. The immediate irony is that by mid-August most kids can't wait for school to start (even the ones who deny it), but I've rarely met a teacher who feels that way.

But we come back early so we can learn to be better teachers. A-hem. I could count on one hand the number of useful insights I've received from inservice training, and on one fist the insights which translated into improved classroom performance.

The school district goes out and hires presenters to teach us during these inservice sessions. We used to have a variety of presenters, but more and more they just herd us into the school auditorium and let one educationist rattle at us. I'm sure there are fiscally prudent reasons for doing this, and I wouldn't complain anyway. It is easier to achieve anonymity in an auditorium audience.

A lady called the curriculum director is responsible for lining up the presenters for our inservice sessions. I don't know where she finds these people but she seems to have two fairly rigid criteria: First, the presenter must hold fast to the tenet that the behavior most to be avoided in the classroom should be modeled during the

20

presentation (i.e., boring instruction); and second, the presenter must speak in a monotone at all times.

Of course, these sessions are highly annoying to the classroom teacher. We know as well as our students when we are not learning anything. So we've devised our coping mechanisms. At the start of each inservice presentation you will see teachers scurry to find seats next to those they feel most comfortable talking with; they will proceed to converse throughout the session, trying to maintain the maximum level of volume which permits hearing without coming across as blatantly rude. (It's a fine line, often crossed.)

Creativity is required of those with a less garrulous nature. My favorite game is surveying the crowd. I give out three awards: The Most Wide-eyed, to that teacher (always a rookie) who actually believes something of benefit is to be derived from the session; The Most Changed in Appearance, to the teacher most unrecognizable after a summer's makeover (the reigning champion is a coach who returned with a gut-splitting perm); and The Most Unmannered, to the teacher who makes the least pretense of listening. (Sleepers and knitters are disqualified. I admire the audacity of headphones.)

Not all presenters are idiots. Some realize immediately that they are dealing with a hostile audience, and the proud but few are even willing to engage the battle. I have grudging admiration for the inservice presenter who will clear his throat into the microphone, or adopt a verbal mannerism that is impossible to ignore (one memorable lady hissed all her s's), or even haul out the nuclear warhead of inservice combat—group involvement activities.

You have to feel a little sorry for these people. After all, it's an ugly job, they only get to do it about once or twice a year, and they can't be paid all that much for it. What is the poor presenter to do? Well, I know what he *shouldn't* do. As a public service, I've formulated *The Eleven Don't's of Doing an Inservice Presentation*. Educationists, take heed!

1) Don't use an overhead projector.
2) Don't lecture for over fifteen minutes.

3) Don't ask anyone to move up to the front.

4) Don't take your audience response personally.

5) Don't use any "touchy-feely" group therapy techniques.

6) Don't forget to bring coffee and donuts (especially coffee!).

7) Don't speak in a monotone.

8) Don't ever plead with your audience.

9) Don't pretend you wish you were still a classroom teacher (we hate that).

10) Don't wake the teachers when they appear to be in REM sleep.

11) Don't read your inservice evaluation forms.

That tells you what not to do, which is kind of like advising a drowning man not to go under and take a deep breath. Could I be more helpful? Probably not. The best advice I got from the School of Education came from a professor who took me aside and told me that most of what he was teaching in Techniques of Classroom Management was folderol. "What matters," he said, "is whether or not you can stand up in front of a class and turn it on. And you can't be taught how to do that."

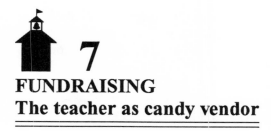

7
FUNDRAISING
The teacher as candy vendor

The teacher two doors down from me sells candy. Snickers. Reese's Peanut Butter Cups. Skittles. (Skittles are very popular.) She sells it at the beginning of each period, and then she begins her daily lesson. She has told me on a good day she will make sixty dollars, and she will rarely bring in less than thirty. This lady is not a capitalistic entrepreneur. She is a junior class sponsor.

Of course, I realize the necessity of fundraising. If students are not allowed to engage in moneymaking projects, how is the dance team going to get money for new uniforms, how is the tennis team going to afford a new ball machine, and how will the Future Farmers of America pay for that trip to the state fair? The taxpayers will have to spring for it, that's how. Read my lips on that one.

Most people have no idea what it costs to be a cheerleader or a member of the dance team. Two years ago a teacher told me she spent $1,700 on her daughter over the course of one year. That covers three or four different dance costumes, a one-week camp in the summer, and a trip to Orlando for some kind of national competition. That doesn't even include the costs defrayed through fundraising!

I acknowledge that most of the money raised by school organizations is used for admirable causes (certainly better than the above!). The Student Council at my school is involved each year in raising money for Project Graduation, a year-end chemical-free party for seniors that is designed to keep them away from alcohol and off the roads. The French Club contributes to Elf Louise, a group that provides toys to needy children at Christmas. I'm barely scratching the surface here.

I will further admit that involvement in fundraising has some educational value for the normal high school student, who learns financial responsibility, salesmanship, and supply-side economics. Fundraisers teach teamwork and working together for a common goal. One look at a team breaking out a new set of warm-ups amply demonstrates the value of a real-life lesson in the rewards of capitalism.

But a sickness has pervaded high school fundraising. For the sake of sustaining some fairly empty traditions, we are denigrating the role of the teacher in order to accommodate the apathy of the modern day student. Take Homecoming. We have a hall-decorating contest among the classes (seniors, juniors, sophomores, and freshmen). We average approximately 300 students per class, and I have rarely seen more than twelve working on a particular hallway. We also have a parade with class floats, and an energy-wasting, environment-polluting bonfire, again with minimum class participation. Obviously, all these things take money.

But what really gets to me is the Junior-Senior Prom, which brings me back to the teacher two doors down. Every year our prom is held at one of the finer hotels on the San Antonio Riverwalk. By the time you consider the rental fee, the food, the programs, the mementoes, etc., you are looking at a $10,000 bill. The juniors are responsible for "staging" the prom for the seniors, and they've been having it down on the Riverwalk for longer than I've been around. To have it at a lesser site would be greeted with howls of derision.

Unfortunately, those twelve students who are willing to pitch in on the hallway decorations are the only ones willing to help in the class fundraising. If each one of those kids manages to raise $100, you have $1,200. That leaves you with a balance of $8,800. Where does the money come from? Enter the junior class sponsor, who is finally responsible to see that all the bills get paid. Of course, nothing sells to a teenage market like candy, so she implores all the teachers with a heart soft enough or tooth sweet enough to sell candy in their rooms. It is a team effort, in a convoluted way—the teacher is reduced to the function of a vending machine, the students are involved in the fundraising to the extent they are willing to rot their teeth for the sake of the cause (most are very willing!), and the educational milieu is transformed into a countinghouse amid a roomful of kids whose blood is throbbing with glucose. But the prom will be beautiful!

Perhaps the problem is extreme at my school, but I haven't been to a school yet that didn't have a problem with fundraising, and candy is the usual solution. It seems clear that some reforms are called for. First, the burden of fundraising needs to be taken off the classroom teacher. That's not our job. Students in any organization need to know that the cost of the activities they want to engage in will be determined solely by their ability to raise the money for them. One or two proms in the high school gym would do wonders in righting the perspective. Secondly, every organization needs to cut back a little. The dance team could get by with two costumes instead of three, and the football team. . . . (Uh oh, I'm getting into sacred cows in Texas.) One thing we teach very little of in the public school system is frugality, a skill which will serve them extremely well in the world they're inheriting.

Finally, we could come up with more creative ways to make money. Schools have barely scratched the surface of ways to involve their very large constituencies in recycling, and there's a great deal of money to be made in that. One group at our school had an aluminum can drive awhile back and came away with a tidy sum. Raising the collective consciousness about the importance of protecting the environment would be a nice secondary benefit, far more valuable than keeping the dentists of America in business.

Let Nestle's and Hershey's and Peter Paul's find someplace other than the schoolyards of America to peddle their poisons. And let the teacher two doors down from me teach.

 **8**

RELIGION
Is there a place in the public schools?

Several years ago we quit praying at my school. Up until then we had begun every school day with a short prayer over the intercom system, usually spoken by a student. The prayers were ecumenical; no specific deity was named and all supplications were bland and in keeping with sound educational goals. I miss them; the kids always stayed quiet during the prayers, and that gave me a chance to get a little more focused. But a parent must have complained, because the prayers ceased at the start of the 1988 school year.

Two years ago a girl from my school went home after sixth period, put a gun to her head, and pulled the trigger. Our principal called a special faculty meeting the next morning and cautioned us to be sensitive and alert, knowing that such a grisly suicide would unleash powerful emotions throughout our school. After the principal spoke, one teacher, a very religious man, stood up and said, "We can't just sit here and let these things go on. Someone has to tell these kids that there's only one answer to their problems, and that answer is Jesus Christ."

Some teachers applauded his heartfelt words; others might have rolled their eyes. I couldn't help thinking what a fine line it is, what a tough call, to keep separate our personal beliefs from our roles as teachers.

I became a Christian when I was 26 years old. Jesus Christ is directly responsible for my desire to do something to help in this world, and indirectly responsible for my choice to become a teacher. When I first became a Christian, I went kind of overboard. A self-proclaimed Jesus freak, I used to stand on street corners on the campus of the University of Missouri and stuff religious tracts into the hands of college students. I saw every conversation I had as a chance to win a convert. I was obnoxious. My family got surly and my old friends avoided me. And I didn't win many converts.

Obviously, I've changed. If I taught the way I witnessed, I wouldn't have lasted a semester in the public schools. Religion is a very touchy issue there. For every parent who complains about school prayer, there's a corresponding parent decrying secular humanism. We can't get through a year without someone demanding to know why our science department doesn't present creationism as an alternative to the theory of evolution. Most of the English teachers discourage their kids from writing papers about abortion or sex education. Most teachers go to great lengths to avoid any mention of s-e-x, which is what half the kids are thinking about most of the time. Warily, we roll along.

But I make no apologies for my faith and do not mind talking about it. In fact, I doubt if a student has made it through my class without realizing I'm a Christian. The history of Western literature is immersed in the Judeo-Christian tradition, so talking about it would be difficult to avoid. The big difference is this—when I talk about it now, it is as something I believe, not as something they're supposed to. I pray most every day in my class. Not aloud, not with my students, but in my heart. The over-the-intercom stuff is the most ineffectual type of prayer anyway. Everything the Bible teaches about Christian character makes me a better teacher. Keeping religion out of school is a joke.

The danger comes in hawking religion, in seeking converts, in espousing a creed. I wouldn't want my children's teachers doing that even if they were in perfect agreement with me, doctrinally speaking. Every teacher is a role model. Everything you believe, even everything you teach, is filtered through how you act. They watch you more than they listen to you. Whatever the cause, whatever the creed, live in a manner worthy of it. As one great book says: "Little children, let us not love in word and in speech, but in deed and in truth." (I John 3:18)

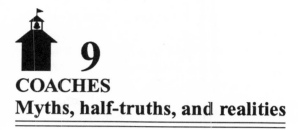

9

COACHES
Myths, half-truths, and realities

Those who can, do.
Those who can't, teach.
Those who can't teach, coach.

—unknown, but probably a teacher

Several years ago I became coach of the high school tennis team. This is my fourth stint as a coach, having previously done junior varsity boys basketball, JV girls basketball, and JV girls volleyball. Obviously, I have never been a bigtime coach, which is all right with me. But I love coaching, and I'm very disturbed by some of the common perceptions of the profession that seem to run rampant in any secondary school, and can best be summed up in the above quote. Here's to a more honest look.

Myth: Coaches can't teach. Of course, there are poor coaches, just as there are poor teachers, and someone who is bad at one will probably be bad at the other. But the characteristics of a great teacher are the same as those of a great coach, and the ingredients for success are the same. Coaching is about motivation and imparting knowledge. Since many classroom teachers feel that motivation is not part of their jobs ("Hey, if the kid won't do the work, it's not my fault if he fails."), the effective coach has a natural advantage in the classroom.

Half-truth: All coaches care about is winning. The most positive benefit a young person can derive from participating in a sport is in the development of his character. Athletics teach discipline, dedication, self-reliance, and cooperation. Most coaches recognize that. But the natural objective of any competition is to win, and winning is the measure of success in our society (sad but true). Furthermore, in many cases a coach has to win in order to keep his job. Coaches have families, desire stability, enjoy recognition—the same as anyone else. If you tell teachers that 90% of their students must make an A in order for the teachers to remain employed, you will see a wide variety of weird classroom practices develop in a very short time.

Reality: Coaches put in longer hours than anybody in the building. Add two and a half hours to the typical school day for after-school practice. On game days, it gets much worse. There are countless details to take care of before a contest, and you can't go home until your last player does. If you play an away game at some distant location, you might not get home until 1:00 A.M., but you're still expected to be in that classroom teaching first thing next morning. Yes, you still have grading, lesson plans, paperwork, and the other time commitments that go with teaching.

There's also the obsession. Anyone who has ever coached can tell about waking up in the middle of the night thinking about a player, a game situation, a technique taught wrong, or a hundred million other details that have to do with the job of coaching. You don't get paid for those hours.

Finally, there's the coach shortage. Since football coaching staffs are typically four to five times larger than any other sport's, if you want to coach basketball or baseball or track, you are also going to be expected to assist with the football team. In Texas a football coach starts working at the end of July, and the football season can last until the week before Christmas (if you are extremely successful). No coaches put in as many hours as football coaches.

Myth: There is a lot of extra money in coaching. My coaching stipend for tennis is $1,400 a year. Considering the time spent (see the above), I would do better with a part-time job at McDonald's. Those coaches who actually make big bucks at it are as rare as writers and actors who do—this is definitely a labor of love.

Half-truth: Coaches don't work as hard as other teachers. (I'll have a lot of coaches up in arms about this one.) I see it like this: My wife likes me to help with dinner—a reasonable expectation. So I do the barbecuing while she takes care of the rest of the meal. When I barbecue, I sit out on the back porch, listen to music, drink a beer or glass of wine, read the newspaper, and flip the meat when it needs it. My wife has a hard time accepting that I'm working as hard on dinner as she is. I argue that just because I'm enjoying it doesn't mean that it's not work. Though I'll never admit it to her, I think she has a point.

Myth: Coaches are not smart. This is an offshoot of the dumb jock syndrome. (Incidentally, the athletes in my classroom are, by and large, better students than the non-athletes.) If you look at the players on a sports team, who is the one most likely to become a coach? The headiest player, the analytical one, the player who studies the game and sees beyond the perspective of his own involvement. In fact, I suspect the great coaches have incredible intellects—but coaches probably come across as boring because they apply their intellect to a very narrow focus. Funny that people don't think of biogeneticists as stupid!

Reality: Coaches teach only so they can coach. My impromptu survey shows that most would leave the profession if they were unable to coach. Mama, don't take my barbecue away.

Myth: Coaching girls is different from coaching boys. Again, I'll get a lot of disagreement on this one, but I think that's just sexism. A coach is striving for the same thing from every player (their best effort all the time), and getting that has nothing to do with the sex of the athlete. Many boys' coaches think girls are too temperamental, or unable to handle constructive criticism (getting yelled at), or unwilling to undergo rigorous physical conditioning. I've got several lazy players on my tennis team, but it doesn't break down according to sex.

Half-truth: Coaches give preferential treatment to athletes. It's probably not as bad as some people think, but I'm sure most coaches look out for the athletes who pass through their classrooms. Part of that lies in two realities previously mentioned: coaches teach in order to coach, and keeping that job often depends upon winning. It is an agonizing thing to lose one of your key players to academic ineligibility. On the other hand, a coach worth his salt is concerned with developing character in his athletes, and you don't build character by teaching people they deserve special treatment.

Reality: Coaches are treated differently by other staff and administrators. Yes, there is a stigma that goes with coaching. I worked at my school for four years before I became tennis coach. I was staggered by how that one change in my position with the school affected how people looked at me. One common assumption was that I would be less concerned with developments that dealt with my job as a classroom teacher. I had become "non-academic." All of a sudden everyone called me coach ("Hey, Coach, how's it going?"). I perceived a subtle difference in my relationship with my colleagues in the English department. Betrayal is too strong a word, but somehow I had let them down. In fact, the non-coaching members of the faculty in general seemed to regard me in a less favorable light, as if I had somehow sold out my integrity as a serious teacher.

I've asked other coaches if they feel the same sort of unspoken disdain, and the answer has almost always been yes. Still, most of them don't care, because the flip side of this is a strong "coaches' fraternity" that regards the rest of the school staff with a frosty belligerence.

Half-truth: Unsuccessful coaches become administrators. I've worked for six different principals, and three of them (actually four; one was a band director—almost a coach) have been former coaches. Most commonly, they got there by getting kicked upstairs. After coaching (usually a major sport) for many years, the coach is unable to maintain the level of success the school has become accustomed to. The powers that be (read: school board) do not wish to reward these years of service with a summary dismissal, but something has to be done to get the ol' team back on the track. Of course, the truly scary thing about all this is that the board is acting on the premise that the success of the team is more important than the success of the school. Go, team, go.

When I became tennis coach, my schedule changed. I now teach three English classes, a freshmen tennis class, and a varsity tennis class. Many of my colleagues make frequent cracks about my cushy schedule, and they have a point. But I think they forget the extra hours my new position requires, and the stress that comes when success is measured by winning and losing, and the altered perceptions of others that come with being a coach. Three years later the stigma remains. Two of our new English teachers were making disparaging remarks about coaches at our lunchroom table. "Hey, watch it," I warned them. "Oh, don't worry," one of them said. "We don't think of you as a real coach." She meant it as a compliment.

10
THE TEACHER AS PSYCHIATRIST
The classroom and the couch

Before I became a teacher, I worked for six years in a mental hospital. That bit of trivia is the recurring inspiration for two rather tired jokes. My students always want to know if I'm *sure* that I *worked* there. My rejoinder is that there really isn't much difference between my old job and my new one.

We both have a point there. One of the life lessons that I carried with me from the mental health days is that it's an extremely fine line that separates the mentally stable from the unbalanced. While working at the hospital I met three people who eventually took their own lives. One was a patient, one was a doctor who became a patient, and one was a staff member who frequently made fun of patients. Furthermore, we had patients who eventually became staff members and vice versa.

Another thing I learned was that adolescence is a combat zone in a war that racks up a pretty fair number of casualties. I remember my own teenage years as being fairly traumatic, and I passed through them relatively unscathed—at least in terms of major upheavals I had to cope with. Yet I can't think about those years without a sort of inward recoiling. So many doubts and confusions and insecurities. And I had it easy.

What major upheavals? In twelve years of teaching I've come

face to face (up close and personal) with the following adolescent traumas: pregnancy, abortion, attempted suicide, suicide, drug and alcohol abuse, physical and sexual abuse, date abuse, extreme poverty, incest, chronic depression, eating disorders, rape, and homosexuality. Surviving such ordeals should earn any good soldier his or her combat pay.

A question I've come up against more than once in the faculty lounge is whether such problems are any of our business. The attitude is not as heartless as it sounds, being most typically expressed in terms of genuine concern: "Look, I'm not trained to counsel someone with their personal problems; I'm trained to teach math [or science or history or even English]. I would probably do more damage than good. If I do become aware that someone in my class has a personal problem, the best thing I can do is pass the information on to someone better equipped to deal with it—like the guidance counselor. Don't you agree?"

No. At least, not necessarily. That mindset creates two problems. First of all, it places no significance on the fact that *you* are the one who became aware of the problem. In my mind that carries a lot of weight. As a rule teachers on the high school level are a sort of natural enemy for students—most of us can walk down a hallway and feel the antagonism. So if we become aware of a student's innermost turmoil, it's usually because that student wanted us to be aware. That's a cry for help. My feeling is that I have been *chosen* (if not by the student, then at least by God). To try and defer that choice would be simple unwillingness to answer the call.

Secondly, to cut myself off from the heart of what is going on in my students' lives would be contrary to my whole philosophy of teaching. I always tell my students at the beginning of the school year that we are going to learn about *more* than English in my classroom—we are going to learn about life. A bit pretentious, perhaps, but I believe it as much as I believe I should be a teacher. If I thought the most important knowledge I was imparting to my students was the identification of adverbial clauses, I'd apply for a job as a garbage collector (I've heard they get paid more). Most of the truly meaningful things that happen in a classroom are only tangentially related to the subject matter being taught.

No doubt we must be careful of how involved we become with our students' personal problems. When a kind ear creates a dependency, the interaction has become counterproductive. I learned rather ruefully in my mental hospital days that I couldn't solve other people's problems for them. Very often the best thing a teacher can do *after* discussing a problem with a student is to refer the student to the counselor, or to pass the information on to someone better suited to deal with it. But in most cases the classroom teacher is the contact point, and we need to be willing to make contact.

Two years ago a student named Dana went home after school one day and blew her head off with a shotgun. Hysteria reigned in our hallways for the next few days, and everyone agreed how shocking and unexpected it was. Our principal handled it well—he got on the intercom and didn't downplay the nature of her death. He said we couldn't allow such things to happen—that we needed to talk to one another and watch out for one another and make sure every person knew that someone cared. The school brought in counselors from the local mental health center to help students deal with their grief. We all had lost someone, and it hurt.

While I grieved for Dana, I thought of Roechelle. I had taught her the previous year, and one of her writing assignments had contained suicidal overtones. I stopped her after class and told her I wanted to talk about it. After initially denying the implications, she came back to me a few days later and admitted she was thinking, almost obsessively, about killing herself. We talked. I arranged for her to see one of the school counselors, who in turn arranged for an evaluation with a psychiatrist. Roechelle ended up missing about three months of school due to an extended stay in a mental health facility.

I saw her just about a week ago. She is a checker at Wal-Mart. It is only a holiday job, and a welcome relief after a harrowing exam week at her university. She pouted because I had selected a shorter checkout lane, but she gave my arm a little squeeze when I passed by.

I like to think I helped save Roechelle. A wall exists in every single classroom of America. The wall is called Authority, and it serves a number of important functions. But it also separates us from our students, and unless we are willing to tear down bits of the Wall, or at least peek over it, we're going to lose more Danas and Roechelles and others. Take a look.

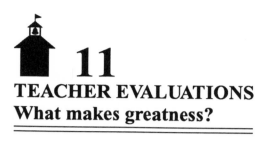

11
TEACHER EVALUATIONS
What makes greatness?

    This year my school district decided I wasn't as good a teacher as I was the year before. They made that judgment on the basis of two visits to my classroom by two different people, one of whom had never seen me teach before. That aggravated me.

    In Texas we use the TTAS—the Texas Teacher Appraisal System—but it happens about the same everywhere. Several times a year someone comes into your classroom with some kind of evaluation "instrument"—gives it a nice surgical sound, doesn't it?—sits there and watches for an hour, and determines how well you teach. The sad thing is that determination often has a significant impact on how well you get paid.

    Since we're talking about money, a closer look at how we get evaluated in Texas is warranted. The TTAS is broken down into six "domains," covering such areas as Instructional Strategies, Classroom Management, and Presentation of Subject Matter. Twice a year (four times if you have less than two years' experience) an administrator comes into your classroom and evaluates your performance in the six domains. Naturally, each of the domains has criteria, and these criteria have "indicators," so-called proof that the desired learning activity is taking place in the class. This gets pretty complex; in fact, the entire instrument totals six pages. So on

Observation Day, along with explaining a lesson to thirty-odd students, you get to think about an administrator and six pages of criteria.

The TTAS is based upon the educational theories of Madolyn Hunter, who claims that all the criteria will happen as a matter of course if effective teaching is taking place. Ms. Hunter is regarded with awe by the educationists, and spoken of in hushed, reverential tones. I don't know if the woman is dead or not. She must be close, judging from the videotape we watched in which she explained her theories.

But back to my plight. The point total of my two evaluations this year gave me an overall rating of *"Exceeds Expectations."* That doesn't sound bad, but my rating for the two previous years had been *"Clearly Outstanding."* If I continue my slide, next year I might end up with *"Meets Expectations,"* which would mean that I really stink. Next thing you know, I'll have to go back to college to learn how to teach.

So I did some investigating. I learned that in our entire district the previous year, there had been 47 perfect scores on the evaluation instrument (I had made one of them). Forty-five of those scores came from the high school. You can imagine the consternation of the administrators from the junior high and the middle school and the three elementary schools and the kindergarten school when they learned that 45 of the 47 most *"Clearly Outstanding"* teachers in the district worked at the high school. Accusations of "creampuff evaluators" were heard behind closed doors. The end result was that I, along with most of my colleagues, wasn't as good a teacher this year. As Dylan said, you don't need a weatherman to know which way the wind blows.

What a joke. No human being can come into my classroom once or twice and make any kind of meaningful evaluation of how well I teach. Why bother? Because we have a public clamoring for accountability, and a legislature searching for "master teachers" they can give extra money to, and administrators who long for a sword. And so we teachers pore over the indicators, choreograph our lesson plans, bribe our students to be good (I'm not exaggerating here; I've heard numerous stories of teachers who have promised their students free pizza, class parties, video movies, or "free days" if the kids would behave during evaluation day), and sweat bullets — all for the sake of a meaningless score.

I've often wondered if it could be done right. Is there any way a teacher's effectiveness can be objectively evaluated? I doubt it. I suppose we'll find out how we really did when we stand before the judgment seat of God, just like everybody else. But there are ways to improve the human process we use to measure our performance.

My first suggestion would be to involve students. They have the only honest picture of how well we are doing our jobs. Like most teachers, I would hesitate to give them too much power in the evaluation process, since they tend to be a bloodthirsty lot. But they ought to have a voice.

Secondly, how well we perform in the measurable ways ought to be a factor. Do we get to class on time? Meet the ticky-tacky responsibilities, like turning in our lesson plans and covering our duty stations and sending assignments to our students in off-campus school? Again, I'd hate to attach too much weight to such things, but they are part of our job.

Finally, we could have some kind of all-star ballot among the faculty. I think I know which teachers in my school are doing the best jobs, and I'll bet most teachers feel the same way. If all teachers were polled, and none allowed to vote for themselves, you might come up with a fairly representative group.

While none of these suggestions is foolproof, I guarantee that some combination thereof would be far more effective in determining a school's best teachers than the TTAS, which seems better designed to determine who is most anally retentive.

Still, the real issue here is what makes a great teacher. I'm reminded of my all-time favorite episode of the Twilight Zone. Donald Pleasance plays a teacher who returns to his school after one summer to learn he no longer has a job. After thirty years of service, he has been put out to pasture. He wanders around campus in a daze, questioning whether his life has had any meaning at all. He winds up in his old classroom with a revolver in his hand, ready to take his own life. Then ghosts start appearing in the desks before him—former students whom he influenced. They tell him about something they learned in his classroom, and how it affected them, and how they went on to have a positive effect on the world around them.

I get all choked up when I watch that show. And that's the only true way greatness can be measured. It's like Christa McAuliffe said: "I touch the future—I teach."

12
CAFETERIA FOOD
Do you know what your kids are eating?

Each year in my sophomore English classes I have my students write an essay about what's wrong with the school. It's supposed to be a persuasive essay—they are to pinpoint a specific problem, identify the audience that can be most influential in solving it, and suggest meaningful steps for corrective action. I tell them if they write effective essays, I will send them on to the intended audience.

Each year I get lots of letters addressed to the cafeteria ladies. I seldom pass them on.

I personally think that institutional food takes a bad rap. You can't hang out at a school, hospital, dormitory, or prison without being overwhelmed by complaints about the food. What do these people expect? You just won't get custom work on an assembly line.

In defense of the cafeteria workers of our nation, and as a rebuttal to hundreds of student essays, I offer the following observations, gleaned from too many cafeteria meals:

1) I have never found an insect in my food.

2) The only things green thus far have been vegetables and Jello.

3) My food has never made any noise.

4) My food has never moved on the platter.

5) My food has never looked like it has been chewed prior to its appearance on my plate.

6) I have never been served the same meal more than three straight days.

In fact, without too much difficulty I can come up with a corresponding list of things I actually *like* about our cafeteria:

1) The food is cheap.

2) They put lots of cheese on everything.

3) They taught me how to make Frito pie.

4) The whole wheat toast is exceptional, as are the salad croutons (made from leftover whole wheat toast).

5) The milk is usually not frozen.

6) Hmmm. Did I mention the food was cheap?

But I too have complaints about lunchtime in the American high school. I'll start with open campus. At my school the seniors are allowed to leave school at lunch and go eat wherever they please. At many schools the privilege is extended to all students, which is probably fairer since I can't think of anything exceptional our seniors do to warrant the special treatment. Still, I don't see the point. Do we really want to promote the idea that kids can get a better meal at McDonald's than at the school cafeteria—where we at least try to maintain the pretense of hitting the four major food groups? The students would stomp and howl if we banned the open campus, but I've seen too many seniors (and others—the class restriction is not well-enforced) sit through fifth period drunk or stoned or otherwise empty-headed (in fact, frequently the chairs are empty) to believe that open campus is furthering our educational ideals.

Speaking of fifth period difficulties, is anything worse than dealing with a hyperactive adolescent who is peaking on the rush of a pure-sugar lunch ingested a half hour earlier? Parents, do you know what your children are eating? Our school cafeteria offers a hot lunch line, a salad bar, a snack bar, two snack machines, an ice cream stand, a popcorn stand, and easy access to soda machines in the boys' and girls' locker rooms. The hot lunch and salad lines are usually the shortest. All this variety is just plain indulgent. A teenager doesn't need to drink anything other than milk (except water—gasp!—sacrilege!), and no one should ever be able to buy his lunch from a machine.

Oh, I could go on. I don't like it that teachers have to pay more for the same lunch than students. It's not like we're independently wealthy in this profession. Being assigned hall and cafeteria duty during lunch is demeaning to a so-called "professional." Our cafeteria seems to rely more and more on plastic and Styrofoam. What are we teaching our students about the environment?

Enough. I'm starting to sound like my students. A few simple steps and the whole problem of cafeteria food evaporates. Be kind to the ladies with hairnets. Eat what they make. Get rid of food machines. Stay in school. If all else fails, fall back on the most pristine of lunchtime traditions—the sack lunch.

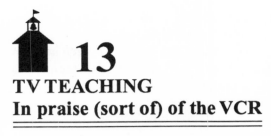

13
TV TEACHING
In praise (sort of) of the VCR

Overheard in an English classroom: "If you people won't sit still and watch, then I'm afraid we'll just have to read the book."

News flash: The most significant technological advancement of the past twenty years in the world of education is *not* the computer. We have three, maybe four, classrooms where computers are used on a daily basis. But in any given classroom on any given day, there's a good possibility that the students are being "educated" by watching the television. Get in line to sign up for the VCR.

When I came to my school six years ago, the library had four televisions/VCR's that could be checked out. Two years ago the library had seven and the English, drama, health, science, social studies, football, basketball, and volleyball programs each had one of their own. Now there is one TV/VCR for every two teachers in the English and social studies departments, and a ton of others. And there are still days when it's hard to get hold of one.

The VCR is an extremely useful educational tool. It can enhance any teacher's presentation of the curriculum. One of my favorite things to do is show the movie *To Kill a Mockingbird* after we have finished the novel. The film won many awards, but in the compare/contrast essay the students have to write, the book always comes out the overwhelming favorite. That's very gratifying.

The VCR also gives us a chance to expose our students to cultural experiences most will probably never sample again. I think

45

it's a tragedy if someone goes through life without ever seeing a Shakespeare play. True, watching it on TV isn't like being there, but it's better than nothing at all. Many a class has been heard to groan, "Is this something from PBS?" only to find themselves absorbed in an interesting program. The people at Public Broadcasting should love VCR's.

One of the best things we can do with a VCR is employ it with a video camera. Any sort of oral presentation will have twice its impact on your students if you allow them to review their performances on videotape afterwards. And giving students control of a video camera allows for the unleashing of unlimited creative potential. We often forget that we're striving for that in education.

The VCR can also be used as a reward and motivator. Sometimes I will let my students watch the film version of a literary work only after they've demonstrated a grasp of the material (i.e., if they do well on the test). A TV show can provide a nice break or variation in the lesson plan when a class has been working too long on one content area.

So, is this a great educational tool or what? Well, not exactly. You see, there's a dark side to the new technology. What the VCR is capable of doing is not necessarily what is being done. Far from it.

I'd say, in our heart of hearts, most teachers would admit that the number one use of the VCR is to keep us from having to teach when we don't feel like it. I will confess to more than a few days when using the VCR amounted to a last-second change in the lesson plan. Maybe I stayed up late the night before. Maybe the copy machine is broken and I can't run off the materials I was planning on using. Maybe I don't feel well. Maybe I just don't feel anything. Now, where can I find a VCR?

Teachers also use the VCR as a kind of academic insurance policy. We know that one major cause of consternation among administrators is the failure rate. We're constantly reminded in subtle ways that we should keep that rate down. Showing the film version of a literary work ensures that our students will have a basic framework for the novel or play—plot, characterization, setting, etc. —even the ones who slept through the reading of the book. It's only a short slide from there to using the film version *instead* of the book (see opening quote).

Some teachers use the VCR as a class babysitter. I knew an English teacher who used to hold film festivals right after her students turned in their research papers. While they sat there entertained (sometimes by films of a decidedly unliterary nature), she'd sit over by the window and get a jump on grading those papers.

VCR's are also effective at controlling a rowdy class. Even if it is a blatant capitulation, a good movie will keep the noise level in most classes at an acceptable level. If you doubt this, check out the VCR sign-up list just before the major holidays — the Wednesday before Thanksgiving, the last day before Christmas or spring break. You had better sign up early. Everyone knows you can't teach kids anything on those days, so the strict teachers give tests and the easy ones show movies.

I have kept a running Hall of Shame for VCR abuses. The all-time record goes to a world history teacher. In a one-semester course, he showed all 13 episodes of *I, Claudius,* the entire *Shogun* (16 hours), and all of *The Winds of War* (23 hours). Over fifty percent of his instruction time was spent watching television. Kids signed up for his class in droves.

A close runner-up would be a summer school class I was partially responsible for. In a summer school course, you are in class for four hours each day. I taught the first semester, and I soon realized it was impossible for anyone (especially those who have failed it once already) to study English four straight hours. Since I had a VCR readily available, I instituted a one-hour movie break, sticking mainly with classics and films with literary value—*Of Mice and Men, The Great Gatsby, Ordinary People.* The teacher who took over the class for the second half continued the practice, but with considerably less discretion. Her class watched *Rambo Part II, Cocktail, Nightmare on Elm Street,* and even *Faces of Death,* a movie Siskel and Ebert called "one of the sickest" they had ever seen. Finding out what had become of my class made me shudder.

It would be fairly simple to make the TV/VCR a positive tool in the educational process. All any teacher really needs to do is ask himself: Am I showing this for the kids' benefit or for mine? If teachers would only check out a VCR when the answer is the former, a VCR would always be available, and our students would be learning from them.

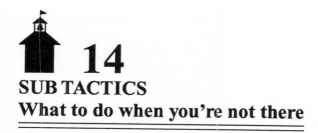

14
SUB TACTICS
What to do when you're not there

I hardly ever get sick, but I am absent a lot. Mostly that's because of my job—the school tennis team is allowed to participate in eight tennis tournaments per year, and most tournaments are played all day Friday and Saturday. That's eight days out of school right there. My administration has also been generous in granting me professional leave in order to fulfill speaking engagements that arise from my writing career. Throw in the rare cold or flu, educational advancement conferences, and personal leave days, and it's not uncommon for me to miss ten to fifteen days of class a year.

I won't apologize for that. My absences are legitimate, an extension of my responsibilities as a teacher and a coach. But I do recognize that my primary responsibility centers on what my students are learning in my classroom, and, given my frequent penchant for not being there, I darn well better make sure that something constructive is going on when I'm gone.

A substitute teacher in my school district is paid $35 a day. That stinks. I have heard they are paid better in other areas of the country ($75 a day in Denver), but I don't think you can count on getting learned, world-wise, compassionate educators as subs anywhere. In Texas they are not even required to have any college hours in order to sub. Even if you get a semi-college-educated sub, the chances of that sub's area of expertise being the same as your own are slim. So it is very unrealistic to think that your replacement is going to be able to provide the same level of instruction as you do when you're there.

So what to do? In keeping with the practical nature of this book, I'm going to help you out. As stated earlier, I've become something of an expert at using subs, and I've developed a set of guidelines that should prove useful.

Find a "steady." I always ask for Norman. Norman knows very little about English. That's okay; that's not his job. Norman likes kids. Norman respects teachers. Norman knows that what he's supposed to do is see that my students fulfill the expectations I have left for them in my absence. Norman will see that the work gets done. Norman will not issue hall passes without a very strong reason. Norman will not allow anyone to run roughshod over him. If I have not done my job adequately and leave Norman with fifteen minutes of dead time when the assignment is over and the bell won't ring, Norman will regale my class with stories of his military background. Find a Norman. (If you don't know a Norman, ask veteran teachers. They'll know.) Then when you call in sick, request Norman. It is also nice to have a back-up Norman.

Be kind to Norman. Don't commit the cardinal sin mentioned above. Ask any sub—the worst classroom situations occur when the teacher hasn't left the class enough to do, and the dreaded "dead time" kicks in. It's completely unfair to expect your sub to come up with a spontaneous lesson plan that fills another fifteen minutes of class time (for $35 a day!). Remember that the responsibility for their learning still lies with you even when you're not there. And please avoid busy work. My kids really hate that. If you're just going to cram worksheets down them, have the decency to be present for the execution.

Make your lessons product-oriented. Your students should have something to accomplish. Even if they're just reading, tack on a little reading check quiz at the end of the hour. They need to be held accountable for what you expect them to do. I think small group, cooperative learning situations (students teaching each other instead of relying on the sub) work fine when you're not there, but the group has to have a goal and a means of proving they reached it. I see nothing wrong with showing videotapes on days when you're absent (even the most unskilled sub can insert a tape and press ("PLAY"), but your students are far more likely to watch and absorb if they know some kind of response is expected of them at the end of the presentation.

Leave your subs what they need. If you're using a VCR, make sure that one is in your room. Leave the videotape, and have it ready at the spot you want your students to begin watching. Leave the necessary items to take roll. Have a seating chart handy. It's extremely demoralizing for the sub to walk in and realize the students have scattered without any means for redress. Leave detailed lesson plans. If your duties extend beyond the classroom (lunch duty, club meetings, etc.), let your sub know. Try to make your instructions positive and upbeat. Dread is the brother of fear, and fear opens the door to chaos. Identify the little darlings most likely to cause problems. Subs don't need to be objective; they need to be warned.

Support your sub, no matter how incompetent. Before you get too judgmental, think back to your own student teaching days. If you sub really stinks up the place, make a mental note never to have that sub in your classroom again. Get a copy of the sub list from the school secretary. But never let your students dictate who your sub is going to be, and take lightly the feedback you get from them on your replacement's adequacy. Most students' idea of great subs are those three little monkeys, see no evil and hear no evil and speak no evil. Except for the boys. There's usually at least one great-looking female college student on our sub list, and that's the one they want.

Me, I'll stick with Norman.

Now that you know what to do with and for a sub, it's okay for you to have one. If you're sick, be sick. Some teachers don't know how to do that. My wife will head for school feeling like death warmed over rather than call in sick. That's partly because she believes no one can instruct her precious ABLE children quite like she does. (She is good.) That's partly because she's just like that; she even approaches housework with a work-till-you-drop vigor. But it's mostly because it's usually more work to plan the day for a substitute teacher than it is to just be there herself. My wife is very thorough.

Last year our school district had an inservice training session on stress management. The presenter came out and said that one of the foundations of proper stress management was making good use of your sick time. She advocated taking "mental health holidays" whenever necessary. The teachers applauded while the administrators up at the front squirmed in their seats. I know a teacher who views using each of the ten sick days we are allotted per year as an inalienable right. She always saves her last one for that long stretch in May when we don't have any holidays. I don't use many sick or personal leave days, but that's because I feel guilty about having so many "legitimate" absences to begin with. I wouldn't hesitate to use one of my days if my physical, mental, or spiritual health needed it.

Most of our illnesses are unplanned, so we don't have the luxury of getting things ready for our sub a day in advance. Instead, calling in sick means dragging yourself out of bed at 6 A.M., fighting off nausea, chills, sniffles, fever, or whatever, and making a sheepish phone call to a suspicious secretary, hoping you sound as sick as you feel. It means driving to the school to throw together the materials to enable your sub to survive and your students to move a little forward, no matter how sluggishly. It means changing or adapting lesson plans so that what you want accomplished can be done with a stranger supervising your charges. No wonder my wife prefers to go to school anyway!

A substitute teacher will never do as good a job in the classroom as a regular teacher, unless the regular teacher doesn't belong there in the first place. It puzzles me why many districts don't realize this and provide their teachers with stronger incentives for not using sick time. I have heard many administrators complain about teacher absenteeism as one of the problems they face. I have heard of rare districts who pay their teachers for their unused sick time, or tie it into an attractive retirement package. It seems like that should be a universal policy. Until it is, if you're sick, be sick.

15
DANGEROUS LIAISONS
The next romance might be your last

Last night I dreamed I made love to the girl in the first seat of the first row. Her parents died when she was younger, and now she lives with one of her girlfriends. She flirts with me a lot, just kidding around stuff, like what am I doing Friday night, and how she doesn't like high school boys. The dream disturbed the hell out of me.

It happens at every high school; at least, I've never worked anywhere I didn't hear about it happening a number of times. A teacher becomes romantically (read: *sexually*) involved with a student, usually with either sordid or tragic results. I've often suspected that some people get into the profession largely because of such possibilities. The fields are ripe, and the harvesters are sleazeballs.

In all of my teacher training, no one has ever said a word about this hazard of the profession. Let me be the first to proclaim it: As a teacher, you will be sorely tempted! Girls go into high school naive and unsure, and they come out lush and voluptuous, and you get to deal with them on a daily basis during the transformation. Many of them have no positive male figure in their lives, and, believe me, they are searching. And your job practically requires that you be witty, self-assured, dynamic, and caring.

54

Incidentally, I have no intention of being sexist about this by limiting it to the male teacher/female student arena. That is merely my own perspective. I've heard enough talk about virile young men from the females in the faculty lounge to know that the high school boy can be every bit as tantalizing as the high school girl.

I'm well aware that true love can happen anywhere, including in the classroom. No one I've ever seen seemed to have very much control over who he fell in love with. Nor does a relationship of such origins necessarily reek of doom. The head of my department married one of her former students, and now they are both excellent teachers. I saw part of a Donahue show once that had teacher/ student marriages, and a few of the couples seemed fairly well-adjusted. Given that the divorce rate in the United States is hovering around fifty percent, a teacher and a student probably have as good a chance as anyone else.

But something ugly turns inside my stomach when I come across a teacher who is obviously on the make. Anyone who has taught knows the type. A science teacher who used to teach across the hall from me would demand a "daily hug" from the two prettiest girls in his class. A coach would have this freshman girl come out and talk to him at his station every single time he had lunch duty. A math teacher had a notorious reputation for showing up at student parties. Even an English teacher became renowned for having daily tutoring sessions after school with a certain handsome male student. And all of them exuded an aura of availability, a certain sexual swagger that sent out a clear if unverifiable message.

My contention is that there's something intrinsically wrong in soliciting, or even accepting unsolicited, the affections of a student in your classroom. Most educators would call it unprofessional. Reprehensible would be more accurate. The teacher has all the power in this situation, and sex and power make a bad combination. Besides the obvious lever of determining the student's grade, the teacher (theoretically) is more emotionally mature, more experienced, and more independent. That makes the student a victim.

Even without the moral imperatives, any teacher who doesn't

strive to keep his hormones in check has a fool for a libido. A teacher I know was arrested in the middle of one of his classes for sexual assault. Handcuffs and all. A student had accused him of groping her after school one day. Although that happened over two years ago and he swore he was innocent, the case is still pending and last time I heard he was working in a convenience store. No administrator is going to be anxious to hire a teacher with a reputation for philandering.

An even bigger fool is the teacher who believes he can pull off such an affair without detection. Schools are greater bastions of gossip than beauty salons. And here's my first maxim of working with teenagers: Never tell a student anything that you are unwilling for the world to know. Usually, the world soon will.

In keeping with my hope that this book would be a practical help to real-life teachers, I've developed a list of specific things to do to avoid potentially awkward entanglements with students. Remember, a good teacher has to be involved, and must relate to his students as a real person. If the alternative to dangerous liaisons is mechanical, faceless instruction, the students have a pretty sorry choice.

Always be aware you're dealing with a very impressionable age. You are the center of attention in your classroom. Any special attention you show will be noticed and, quite possibly, misinterpreted. One thing all students hate is a teacher who has favorites—yet, it's impossible not to have them. Hide them in your heart. Let fairness rule.

Show yourself in a context bigger than the students' limited perceptions. I keep pictures of my wife and three children in prominent places in my classroom. I talk about our lives. I never allow my students to think my life revolves around them.

Be careful *who* and *how* you touch. Touching is an effective teaching device. It secures attention, shows acceptance, diffuses hurt or anger, and communicates affection. It is also sexually potent. I almost always touch by patting on the shoulder, I try to touch boys as much as girls, and I stop touching anyone who responds too eagerly to it. Remember, we can touch their lives without necessarily touching their bodies.

Be aware of your own weakness. Certain people in your classroom could fuel the flames of a thousand sexual fantasies. Indulgence is the first step on the pathway to surrender. The urge is the father to the deed. Cold showers and pure thoughts are the best prescriptions.

Avoid compromising situations. Conduct conferences and tutorials with your door wide open. Be careful of extracurricular activities that provide opportunities for you to be alone with a student for extended periods of time. Try to have a third party present. To quote the Bible: Avoid any appearance of evil.

I've always admired Jimmy Carter's admission in the famous *Playboy* interview that he still had "lust in my heart." Don't we all? The vast majority of teachers would sooner jump into a lake than into an affair with a student. But it happens, over and over and over. Our responsibility extends beyond simply not doing it ourselves. These situations don't develop in a vacuum. A few words of prevention could be worth several tons of heartbreak. Speak them. Heed them.

16
MARRIED TEACHERS
With this job, I thee wed

Most married couples would view the prospect of working together, or sharing the same occupation, with a combination of horror and hopelessness. I've asked around about this. Men seem to feel that job and marriage mix like oil and water. Women have similar reservations; to many, the workplace represents a declaration of independence from the confining roles of wife and mother. They have no interest in bringing along excess baggage. Both agree that being forced to share most of a twenty-four hour day together would spell certain doom for the marriage.

Some school districts share this theory of the dangers of too much togetherness. A district which borders mine has a strict policy of not hiring spouses. My old district was willing to hire them as long as they did not work at the same school.

My current district has no such policy. Right now there are four married couples who teach at the high school. All have been married as long as I've been there, and none of the marriages seems to be foundering or showing signs of strain. In fact, the relationships appear quite vital. Come to think of it, our superintendent is married to an English teacher in my department. Wouldn't it be something if she got called before the school board?

As I glance over a list of our faculty, I'm amazed at how many teachers have spouses who are also involved in public education. I think these people have stumbled onto something. Teaching couples have some built-in advantages to their relationship which, if bottled, could perform wonders in lowering the divorce rate.

The most obvious advantage is financial. Marrying a teacher allows you the luxury of being able to afford to teach. (I vowed when I began this book that it would not evolve into a diatribe demanding better pay for teachers.) No one gets into teaching to make big bucks. The sad truth is many good teachers get out because of the minimal financial rewards. You simply cannot raise a family on a teacher's salary. However, you can on two teachers' salaries.

Another advantage married teachers share is an emotional one. Teaching brings its own special set of stresses. Bad days are as inevitable as death and taxes, only far more chronic. If the kids don't get you, the bureaucracy will. So early in any teacher's career, she learns to commiserate. What a comfort it is to go home to a first class commiserator! Of course, if you both had bad days . . .

Teachers have time for each other. That's not to say you won't be busy—you will work long hours, you will bring work home with you. Any teacher worth her red pen works a fifty-plus-hour work week. But you will work the same hours, and, gloriously, you will have the same time off. Weekends. Most major holidays. Two weeks at Christmas. Spring breaks. And, most of all (in hushed, reverential tones)—summers. Naturally, this advantage assumes that you want to spend time with your spouse.

The fourth advantage grows right out of the third. More time with your spouse means more time with your children. I'll be unequivocal about it: No job is better suited for raising a family. I know every child that my children play with. Heck, I've played with most of them myself. There isn't a father in the neighborhood who spends more time with his kids, and I'm competitive with most mothers. I decided very early on that I wasn't going to look up one day and find my children all grown up, and wonder how they got there. Bethany is fourteen now, Nathan's twelve, and Zachary's ten. I could expound on every stage of their development (I'll spare you). On most days they'll admit they've liked having me around.

Of course, there's a downside to marrying another teacher. In a sense, you never really get away from your job. You can't expect her to listen to your tales of woe if you won't listen to hers. And you'll never be rich.

But I think the greatest benefit of marrying another teacher, the tie that binds your relationship together, is a spiritual one. I have taught for twelve years. For the first eight of those years, my wife stayed at home to raise our children, picking up a wide variety of part-time jobs to cover the shortfalls in my salary. Then she became involved in special education as a classroom aide, and this year will be her second as a classroom teacher. The thing is, we both feel good about what we do. There's a lot to be said for that. So many of the kids I teach want to become accountants or radiologists or corporate executives, and when I ask why, the answer inevitably boils down to a material goal. That doesn't do it for me. I love being a writer, and I'm very proud to have had books published. But at the gates of heaven, the first thing I'll say is that I was a teacher. Won't get me in, but it sure can't hurt.

17

WHO'S IN CHARGE
The class clown—is it you?

I went back to college to become a teacher when I was twenty-nine years old. During my first year of real-life teaching, I came home about half the time convinced that I had made the wrong decision about what to do with my life. I taught three classes of seniors, and all of my ideals about conveying the nobility of learning, and making education enjoyable, and preparing young adults for the future were soon shattered.

My misery reached its peak one day when I hauled the class clown out of my classroom. I shut the door behind me, got up in his face, and chewed him out. He stood listening, cross-armed, a languid grin playing across his face. Anger and hopelessness overwhelmed me as I realized nothing I said made the least bit of difference to this young man. Turning back to the classroom in disgust, I yanked on the doorknob. It was locked. My school had the old-fashioned doors with the glass panes framed in the top half. I looked across the classroom at my desk—my keys were lying on the blotter. I looked at my students—they were smiling broadly. I rapped on the door and the smiles turned into laughter. No one moved. In the reflection of the glass pane, I could see the class clown behind me, mugging for his classmates. As I began to dissolve into a puddle of embarrassment, one of the more compassionate girls in the class got up from her seat and came and opened the door. That class was a lost cause for the rest of the year.

I am not a great disciplinarian, but I have learned (painfully) that if you don't establish discipline in your classroom, you won't establish anything else.

Most beginning teachers understand this quite well. I would say establishing classroom discipline is their number one source of anxiety as they begin their jobs. Many tend to err in one of two ways.

The first is the military mindset approach. You are the drill instructor, they are the raw recruits. Be rigid, be inflexible. Dare them to challenge your authority. Rule through fear and intimidation. I once received the following piece of advice: "On the first day of school, the very first time any kid acts up, in any way whatsoever, walk over to your wastebasket and kick it across the room. You won't have another discipline problem for the rest of the year." Well, maybe. But I can picture the conversation at a student's dinner table. "What did you learn from your psycho teacher today, son?"

The real problem with the military mindset is that it's no fun. You establish control at the cost of communication. Young people can be forced to obey, but they cannot be forced to express themselves. And how is the teacher affected? Wearing a sour expression on your face all day will soon translate into a sour life. You can find examples in any faculty lounge.

The second approach goes to the opposite extreme. I call it the social worker syndrome. You are going to reach your students and change their lives. You're determined to relate to them. You will be their friend. You respect their right to learn at their own rate, and you encourage them to express their own individuality. Sounds wonderful, doesn't it? While it elicits more sympathy from me, the social worker syndrome is probably even less effective than the military mindset.

Some of the best advice I ever got about teaching came from a guy who told me to find my friends someplace other than my classroom. That doesn't mean you can't associate with them apart from your roles as teacher/student. I've gone golfing, played tennis, and even had barbecues with people I've taught. What it does demand is that you always maintain a decorum that you wouldn't find necessary with a friend.

Of course, teachers blame undisciplined students on the parents. Rightfully so. It is ridiculous to expect a high school teacher to do in 180 hours what a parent has been unable to accomplish in fourteen years. Still, maintaining discipline in the classroom is not a matter of moral reclamation—it is a matter of survival.

So here's the survival primer; practical advice for establishing and maintaining discipline in your classroom:

1) Be prepared — just like the Boy Scouts, numero uno, before all things. You must have something for them to do. Whoever came up with that one about idle minds and satanic workshops had it right.

2) Be consistent — if you're not consistent, they won't believe you. If they don't believe you, every threat is empty, and every situation becomes an incident. It's soon after that you drown.

3) Be personal — this gets tricky, but it's important. Remember that you're dealing with an individual. Treat him as such. Find out what is going on in his life. If he believes you care, an enemy can become an ally.

4) Use anger judiciously — one time I swept the textbooks off my desk and into the trashcan. One time I shattered my chalk on the opposite wall. Yes, I even kicked the wastebasket once. But those kind of histrionics only work when used discreetly. And the bottom line is to always control your anger. When it controls you, the next step is to change careers.

5) Document and contact — keep a discipline log. Better yet, have the student write something explaining his role in the disciplinary incident. Go over it. When it gets to the

point of contacting the parent, you will have ready ammunition. Seldom will contacting a parent have any effect on classroom behavior, but it's a necessary step in the process of removing a chronic offender from your classroom permanently.

6) Follow up — don't let the administration let you down. One time I sent a kid to the office for misbehaving. I don't do that often, so when I do, it's supposed to mean something. He came back smirking. "Mr. Fennell [the assistant principal] says I have to apologize," he said. "Sorry." "That's not good enough," I announced. "Come with me." I marched him back down to the assistant principal and demanded a stiffer penalty. I got it.

Which brings me to some advice for administrators: Back us up. Plain and simple. Let every student in the school know that the administration believes in its teachers. Not that teachers are infallible. I'm sure that some teachers' ineptitude, especially in disciplinary matters, must drive administrators crazy. But that has to be dealt with privately, and the student should not be privy to it. I also strongly advocate that disruptive students be removed from the classroom setting. One student can prevent a whole class from learning anything—and take great pleasure in doing it. That shouldn't be allowed to happen.

Learning works best in a classroom when discipline becomes a nonissue. That's not as difficult to accomplish as it might seem. It only requires that a teacher communicate his expectations regarding classroom behavior to his students, be consistent in insisting those expectations be met, and intervene immediately when they are not. To quote the Nike commercial, just do it.

 **18**

SMOKING: WHERE? WHEN? WHO?
The Texas/Utah conflict

The bathrooms in my school are disgusting. No one seems to take any particular aim at the urinals. The packages of toilet paper are customarily dropped into the toilets whole, where they soak up water and expand into bloated, untouchable rolls. We have graffiti that would make Two Live Crew blush. Nothing affords a more explicit view of the depraved nature of the American teenager than a cursory examination of a high school john.

If we didn't have private facilities for the faculty, I just wouldn't go. I swear I wouldn't. I suspect my sentiment is shared by countless others less fortunate than I, and if you look closely in any classroom you can detect the imperceptible facial tics that accompany the struggle for the self-attainment of a state of constipation. Those souls deserve respect.

Of course, the bathrooms are the last bastion for the students who want to smoke. Their "legalized" smoking area was taken away from them years ago. Now, walking into the restroom in between classes is like stepping into a Mad Max movie.

One time last year, feeling a sense of authoritarian duty, I walked into the boys' bathroom to chase the smokers away. As soon as I opened the door, the hushed warning "Teacher! Teacher!" passed quickly through the room. I moved slowly through the

65

smoke and the sleaze, not challenging the hard, confrontational stares I got from the inmates. In the last of four stalls three kids stood around the toilet, which had three cigarette butts floating in the water.

"My, this looks cozy," I said sarcastically. "You guys must have had to go really bad."

Just then the lights went out. The room was pitch black, the switch was all the way over by the door, and I was a stranger in a hostile land!

"All right, turn on that light!" I said in my sternest voice.

"F___ you!" someone responded.

"Stupid c_____!" someone else agreed.

I moved blindly in the direction of the door, bumping into a body that bumped back even harder. My hip knocked against a sink. I stepped forward again, more forcefully.

"Hey, watch it!" someone said angrily.

To my right I saw a faint patch of light on the ground. I remembered that our bathroom doors had vented bottoms, and I lunged that way, using a straight arm that would have done Emmitt Smith proud. I flicked on the switch by the door.

"Everybody out! This bathroom is closed," I said, trying not to sound distressed. The rabble filed past me, most of them grinning sardonically.

It's not a very popular position, but I favor having a designated smoking area. That does not mean we are condoning the habit—not at all. We are morally responsible to teach the students in their health classes (a required course) what the effects of smoking cigarettes are. But in high school we are working with young adults—taking young people and teaching them to be adults. You have to bring a certain respect for free will into that mix. I've talked with lots of foreign exchange students over the years, and the European students are always astonished to learn that we try to dictate whether our teenagers can or cannot smoke. Besides, the pragmatist in me insists that we're never going to eradicate this problem, and the situation in the bathroom really is intolerable.

And if I were a student, I'd be a bit peeved about the way the system works. A teacher can walk into the restroom, catch them smoking, and haul them down to an assistant principal, who will assign them to Saturday school or some form of detention. In the meantime the arresting teacher can go down to the faculty lounge, light up a smoke, and brag about busting another one. The hapless students become victims of the age-old hypocrisy—do as I say, not as I do.

Our faculty lounge is divided into two sections separated by a glass wall, one side for smokers, one for nonsmokers. The two sections have been dubbed Texas (smokers) and Utah (nonsmokers). No one knows the origin or reason for these names, but they are accepted as a matter of course. The lounge is peopled by three types: the ardent smokers, the zealous nonsmokers, and the ambivalent (or apathetic) 'tweeners, who are permitted safe passage on both sides. I fall into the third category, being an ex-smoker who has a great deal of respect for the goddess Nicotine.

The school board, ever at the forefront in the war against hypocrisy (ho ho ho), has recently decreed that all smoking will be banned on all campuses beginning next year. This pronouncement was greeted with vigorous (sanctimonious?) approval in the Utah lounge, and with a flurry of inquiries into other job possibilities on the Texas side. Like the fighters at the Alamo, the Texans have known they were doomed for several years. Now the bell is tolling.

All this gives rise to an interesting ethical dilemma: What do we do when we catch someone smoking in the restroom, only to discover that the offender is one of our colleagues?

Turn out the lights, the party's over.

Addendum: We are just finishing up our first year as a smoke-free campus. Overall, I have to approve. I can't say that we have dramatically improved the smoking-in-the-john problem, but at least we don't feel so hypocritical when we bust a student for it. The glass partition still exists in the faculty room, but both sides look like Utah now. Certainly it has been a struggle for some of my colleagues. As tennis coach, I have an office, which is really an old, windowless storage room in the back of the building near the tennis courts. A few teachers have made overtures, inquiring into the possibility of acquiring a key to my office. No chance, I told them. So now, everyday, during a conference period, or at lunch, or even in between classes, you'll spot certain Texans heading out to their cars in the teachers' parking lot, slipping inside them, maybe even taking a lap or two around the school grounds. Wonder what they're doing out there?

19
STRIP GRAMMAR AND OTHER DIVERSIONS
C'mon, take a chance

Martin Luther King, Jr., said, "Human salvation lies in the hands of the creatively maladjusted." That inspires me.

I'm not much for teaching grammar, and I teach next door to the greatest grammar teacher in America. Margaret Palmer. Every now and then I can hear her shriek out, "What does the participle modify? Why are you dangling it!" or "Tut tut! Check your pronoun antecedent agreement." She gets excited about it. Here's how good she is—her sophomores learn the rule of polite request. That's when you state something as a question but you really don't mean it as a question, you mean it as a command, so you use a period instead of a question mark. Like "Would you please be quiet."

I never heard of that rule until I was thirty-nine years old and she told me about it. I still don't use it, but I love Mrs. Palmer. I'd feel guilty if I didn't teach any grammar at all, so several times a year we pull out the blue Warriner's textbooks and knock down a few chapters. The going gets rough. The kids sense my lack of enthusiasm for the subject, and I don't believe they're going to retain anything of real value anyway. But we do it, and once or twice a class period I get asked, "When are we going to be finished with grammar?" (Should I omit the question mark? Arrrgghh!) Sometimes I want to do something to liven it up.

That's how I invented Strip Grammar. It's easy to play. We just go through a grammar exercise with me calling on people, and whoever misses has to take something off. If the students get five straight correct, I have to take something off. I know this game sounds dangerous, but it's harmless. No one gets called on more than two or three times in a class period, and anyone can "take off" a ring or an earring, a shoe or car keys or a wallet. But I promise it holds their interest, especially when I call on the prettiest girl. Some of the bolder guys will whisper the wrong answer to her while the others just hold their breath. Of course, some miss intentionally, and I usually have at least one hot dog who immediately starts to strip off his shirt. I don't mention this game in the faculty lounge; some people wouldn't understand.

The best teachers do take chances. They experiment with different approaches to what they are teaching, and they incorporate what works and discard what doesn't. They know the biggest enemy they face in the classroom is boredom. The bored student drifts off and learns nothing. It amazes me how many teachers allow students to sleep in their classroom, as if relieved at not having to deal with another point of consciousness.

Admittedly, many factors discourage us from being innovative or original. The status quo carries a great deal of weight in the public school system. Even our teacher evaluations are formulaic, encouraging all teachers to teach in a certain way in order to score well. Since we work with young and impressionable minds, we don't know how what we do is going to be explained and interpreted at home. (I've never had a call about Strip Grammar—I'm astounded!) Most administrators would choose a mind-numbing traditional approach over a controversial experimental one. In a second. And teacher jealousy can be a stumbling block. I still think I lost a job once because my unconventional methods and subsequent popularity with my students raised the dust on a veteran teacher.

Still, doing things differently keeps us young and keeps our students involved. My students look forward to coming to my class.

That gives me confidence and stimulates me to keep looking for new things to try. Sometimes the results are extraordinary.

Several years ago I was teaching the novel *Lord of the Flies* to my sophomores. The plot concerns a group of boys who become stranded on a tropical island during a war. No adults are with them, and they have to fashion their own form of civilization, which very quickly deteriorates into anarchy and barbarism. After the third chapter, I announced to the class I would no longer be teaching the book. I would go and sit in the corner as a symbol of the book's "Beastie in the jungle." They had one week to finish the novel and prepare for the test. How they did that was completely up to them—no adult intervention.

I watched my own "Lord of the Flies" unfold in fascination. In one class two girls tried hard to structure an orderly society. They prepared a reading schedule, wrote study questions, and demanded full class participation. Some students rebelled, refusing to take them seriously and breaking off into their own private conversations. The next day the girls came in with a new seating chart, one that separated every student from the friends they'd most like talking with. They almost pulled it off. Finally, a boy stood up and said, "I ain't gonna sit here," glancing warily at me. Like the Beast, I remained silent. Within moments order had dissolved and all the students had moved to wherever they pleased. By the end of the week, even the two girls chatted happily with no semblance of studying the book.

Another interesting result of the experiment was the effect it had on me. Remaining silent in the corner as my class slowly sank into chaos and disorder required all my patience and resolve. On the second day a teacher came in to ask me about something. She gave me a funny look when she noticed my class didn't seem to be doing much of anything. She came back into my class on the fifth day. Now there was no semblance of any type of learning going on. I couldn't stand it! "This isn't the way I usually teach," I explained quickly. "This is an experiment. Honest. I'd never let my class act like this." She still looked at me funny.

Predictably, the test scores on the objective test were pretty low. But when they got to the essay question where I asked them to draw parallels between what happened on the island and what happened in our classroom, light bulbs clicked on. I got some wonderful student writing. And I still have kids from those classes mention *Lord of the Flies* when I run into them out of school.

Teachers who take chances are the ones most likely to get irate phone calls from parents. They're the ones most likely to get called down to the principal's office. They're the ones most likely to get fired. They are also the ones most likely to succeed.

 **20**

THE TEACHER IN HOLLYWOOD
Look what they done to my job, Ma

Hollywood doesn't like teachers. If an alien was sent to earth to learn about our profession by studying everything on film about us (hey, do I have a movie plot here?), he'd come away with an impression that would leave him holding his alien nose. Maybe it's because people involved in the arts tend to be rebels.

Maybe it's because the most exciting, heroic things teachers do don't translate very well to film. Maybe it's because half the people in Hollywood are high school dropouts (my personal suspicion). Or maybe it's because the movies are just a reflection of the popular taste, and the public doesn't like us very much either.

Whatever. As our alien watched the celluloid roll by, he'd become convinced that teachers are sleazy little lechers. (Who can forget the scene from *American Graffiti* where Richard Dreyfuss's former teacher offers him worldly advice before being pulled away by a nubile coed?) Teachers have no control over their classrooms. (In *Fast Times at Ridgemont High,* Sean Penn has a pizza delivered to him in class while his teacher watches helplessly.) Teachers are self-aggrandizing bastards. (Coach Craig Nelson takes extreme measures to deprive player Tom Cruise of attaining a football scholarship after Cruise refuses to play dirty in *All the Right Moves*.) Teachers are disgusting, immoral, sadistic pigs. (See any scene involving the P.E. teacher in the *Porky's* series.)

Or our alien might want to expedite matters by selecting a movie tellingly titled *Teachers*. In this one film he would learn that high schools routinely graduate illiterate students, that it's possible for a teacher to fall over dead in a classroom without being noticed for days, that the most sensitive, caring teacher is the one who gives a girl a ride to the abortion clinic, and that the most effective teacher is an escapee from a mental hospital. What is our alien to think?

But the Lifetime Achievement award for teacher-bashing goes to that legendary maker of adolescent films, John Hughes. Ah yes, *The Breakfast Club.* Five young people struggling to find their identities are assigned a Saturday D-hall under the tutelage of one teacher. The teacher is alternately insulting, tyrannical, apathetic and self-serving. The students roam the hallways, vandalize the school, smoke pot, dance on the library furniture—and find themselves. When they need some positive, adult feedback, they go to the janitor. Fast forward to *Ferris Bueller's Day Off.* Ferris plays hooky, becomes world famous, outsmarts every adult he meets, fixes his best friend's relationship with his father, and grins smugly at the camera. The school's assistant principal spends the day obsessively trying to prove that Ferris is truant. Ferris finishes the day in triumph, the educator in abject humiliation. Fast forward to *Some Kind of Wonderful.* Lea Thompson talks her way out of a D-hall by shamelessly flirting with the driver's ed teacher, even going so far as to compliment him on his smooth hairstyle. (The teacher is bald!) Fortunately for us teachers, our little alien is apt to discover at the John Hughes' Film Festival that his misogyny extends beyond teachers and embraces the entire adult population.

I know that most of these films are meant to be comedies, and teachers, like everybody else, should be able to laugh at themselves. But I believe the movies have a cumulative effect, and that effect bodes no good for us. Right now we are struggling to attract better people into our profession, to increase community support and involvement, to raise our salaries. All of these objectives are directly dependent on the public's perception of what we do. We'd be fools to underestimate Hollywood—it exerts more influence on people's thinking than any other media source. Just walk into a video store and see how many movies are checked out. With the advent of VCR's, everybody sees everything. And what they see about teachers is usually negative.

But not always. While it's certainly a rare event for Hollywood to make a meaningful picture about teaching, it does happen. The result can be downright inspirational. So next time you feel lost in a video store, check out one of the Five Greatest Teacher Movies Ever Made (I originally intended to have ten movies on the list, but alas . . .):

Dead Poets' Society—the most recent, and one of the best. Robin Williams shows us what vibrancy can do in a classroom, and how our real job is not just to fill heads, but to affect lives. It made me feel proud to be a teacher.

Stand and Deliver — teaches us how all personality types can be effective teachers. Edward James Olmos is a low-key math teacher with an unshakeable faith that his inner city Hispanic students can learn calculus. He combines that faith with unfailing dedication to the task of teaching them. This movie showed me I needed to work harder.

Children of a Lesser God — a moving romance, but the very best scenes occur in the classroom. William Hurt puts the "special" in special education as he teaches in a school for the deaf. Hurt accepts every student for what he/she is, but is never content to leave one there. The film is a two-hour public service announcement for using creativity in teaching.

To Sir With Love — illustrates how teaching can be a calling. Sidney Poitier throws out the curriculum and makes education relevant to working-class London teenagers, all the while seeking a better job for himself. His students learn self-respect, and Sidney learns about himself, too. Don't miss his dance scene.

The Prime of Miss Jean Brodie — required viewing for any teacher feeling ineffective. No one has more influence upon her students than Maggie Smith. You might despise her by the end of the film, but you will know you've watched a master teacher at work.

While I'm not willing to expand my list, I would offer honorable mentions to *Goodbye Mr. Chips, Up the Down Staircase,* and *Conrack.* If we could keep that alien spy glued to those eight films, teachers might be able to assume their rightful position in the intergalactic scheme of things.

21

THE DREADED PHONE CALL
Talking to parents

In the eleventh grade I struggled with geometry. Actually, the class wasn't that tough, but I was easily distracted. One day the teacher gave us a class assignment and paced around the room as we got to work. I lost interest after a bit, so I leaned forward to talk to the girl in front of me. *Smack!* The teacher came up behind me and slammed me across the back of my neck with a yardstick. I must have shot three feet out of my chair. I landed with my fists clenched, and the teacher smiled at me, daring me to take a swing at him.

If I had gone home and told my parents what the teacher had done, they would have congratulated him for his disciplinary technique and extended the punishment at home. If I did today in my classroom what that teacher did back then, I'd have a lawsuit slapped on me before the red mark came up on the student's neck. The times they have a-changed.

There's a new breed of parent out there today, and every teacher needs to be prepared to deal with them. Contacting parents for both academic and disciplinary problems has become an imperative. It is a teacher's best protection against future reprisals when doing our job means putting "little Junior" in a less than favorable light. Whether our radical action involves a disciplinary referral to the office or a failing grade, if mom and dad are caught unawares there will probably be some squawking. And when parents squawk, principals listen. Anytime you are put into a position of conflict with a student where it is necessary to bring in an administrator, the best way you can begin your defense (and it very often is a literal defense) is "When I spoke to the parents about this . . ."

Having said all that, I'll confess that I'm terrible about contacting parents. It's just something that I hate to do, like grading research papers and taking lunch duty. Mostly, I guess I resent it. I teach high school students; they are supposed to be young adults, entering that phase of their lives when they take responsibility for their own actions. Calling a parent seems so regressive.

Parents are hard to reach nowadays. The odds of getting hold of a parent from school, when the matter is fresh in your head, are slim. That means you have to call in the evening, and even then there's a good possibility the parents (or single parent, more likely) won't be home. Oftentimes you end up talking to the student, who caused the trouble in the first place.

If you do get hold of the parent, the call is usually unpleasant. Naturally, you try to be conciliatory, which usually means you have to be dishonest. Just once I'd like to say, "Your kid behaves like a selfish, spoiled, apathetic, ill-mannered little moron in my classroom. Now where do you suppose he learned that behavior?"

Finally, chances are the call will do very little good. Even the parents who express a genuine concern seem to have no control over their children's study habits or behavior patterns. Contacting parents is time-consuming, frustrating, and usually pointless.

But we still have to do it. It boils down to being at peace with your own conscience. If I know I've gone the extra step with a student, then I can accept his failing my class, or being suspended from school, or whatever. And part of that extra step is calling his parents.

Every veteran teacher has horror stories about contacts with parents. An art teacher friend was pushed up against a wall while she was pregnant because she wouldn't change a failing grade which made some dear man's son ineligible for football. (The art teacher doesn't do parent conferences anymore without an administrator present.) A lady once brought her own college professor to a parent-teacher conference to help argue about her daughter's research paper grade. I once had a parent ask me what was more important, if his son could read and write or if he had a high school diploma. He wasn't joking.

Of course, every parent is different, but there are certain types you can anticipate. If you learn to recognize them, it makes it easier to deal with them. Here's a preview:

1) The "perfect child" parent — Easy to spot. Whatever the situation, the child will not be in the wrong, and if the child is in the wrong, it will be easily explainable. Expect such phrases as "But she didn't understand that . . ." and "He's just growing up a little . . ." and "After you know her better, you'll realize . . ." Recommendations: don't be overly critical, stick to your guns, spell out expectations clearly, take two aspirin after conference.

2) The "overly concerned" parent — Agrees with everything you say. Professes determination to right the path of the child. Assures you of their complete support. In many ways this is the most pleasant type of parent to work with, but there is a pitfall. The parent will ask you to call every time there is an assignment missing, or any difficulty whatsoever, Thus, the burden of correction is placed on you rather than the child. Set up a system in which the child is responsible for reporting to the parent.

3) The "lost hope" parent — Freely admits her own inability to deal with the child. Characterized by the phrase "I can't do anything with him." Seeks to elicit your sympathy, subtly pushes all responsibility off on you. Gives you a free hand in prescribing corrective measures. Only one phone call is necessary.

4) The "on the edge" parent—Always the scariest to deal with (see art teacher). Explosiveness is always palpable in the conversation, and it is difficult to tell where it will be directed—toward child, you, or self. Be extremely cautious in conference, avoid any type of confrontation, make conference brief, and suggest (if necessary, initiate) outside help.

Do I paint a bleak picture? That's because most parental contacts are initiated due to problems. If everything was rosy at home, there would not be a problem in your classroom. (Incidentally, on those rare occasions when I find the time, I will call parents to tell them how well their children are doing. I should do that more often. The parents love it, and it makes me feel good.) Because of such volatile conditions, calling a parent is sometimes like playing hide-and-seek with a rattlesnake. That's fitting, because teaching students can be hazardous to your health. Proceed with caution.

22

SEX, DRUGS, AND SNEAKERS
Are kids getting worse?

What greater or more beneficial service can I render to the republic than to teach and train the youth, considering how far astray our young men have gone because of the prevailing moral looseness. The greatest effort will be needed to restore them and point them in the right direction.

—Cicero (44 B.C.)

I take great comfort from the above quote. How pleasing it is to think of young hoodlums terrorizing a classroom in 44 B.C.! I wonder if they had gangs? Brought weapons to school?

Are kids getting worse? I shouldn't make light of the question, because its implications are enormous. If young people throughout the ages are on some sort of downward continuum, the world is doomed. Our efforts as teachers are stopgap at best, and essentially meaningless. Our jobs will get worse and worse. We face a future without hope.

Evidence indicates they *are* getting worse. I have yet to meet a teacher with more than ten years' experience who feels the students she works with today are better than the ones she had when she began. Everything we are told confirms this. Dropout rates are up, teenage pregnancies are soaring, standardized test scores are down, random acts of violence are commonplace. High school teachers are criticized for the product we are turning out. Look at our raw materials.

Sadly, my own experience corroborates all this. I teach at a suburban school with a military base nearby, so our student population is probably more disciplined and less rebellious than most. But the erosion is indisputable. I don't assign as much homework

81

now, because it's not uncommon for less than half my class to do a particular homework assignment. I hear more profanity in the hallways, from boys and from girls. Certainly I get less respect, and I don't think my teaching methods have changed measurably. In the past few years, gang activity has become a cold reality at our school, and students have been sent home for wearing "colors," defacing school property with gang graffiti, and even bringing weapons to school.

Here's another curious phenomenon: I've noticed an increase in the number of psychologically disturbed youngsters in my classroom in the past several years. Now, I'm no psychiatrist so perhaps that's a subjective judgment, but I trust my instincts. There's a general sense of foreboding I get around certain teenagers, and that sense is tingling more often these days.

If kids are getting worse, then why? It doesn't take an M.S.W. to come up with some answers. The finger points first to the home. The world of Beaver Cleaver is dead. Both parents are more than likely at work when Junior gets home, and they're both too tired to give him much attention when they do get home. If they get home. So many students are from single parent homes that I don't ask mom-and-dad questions anymore.

They face different social pressures, too. Designer labels rule the world. It has to be Nike or Reebok or Girbaud or Cavarrici or Guess? or Umbro or whatever else becomes suddenly hot. We've all heard stories of kids being beaten senseless and robbed of their sneakers or jacket. Those labels cost big bucks. For those unwilling to maim to obtain them, that means a job along with an education. Throw in a few extracurricular activities and who has time to study?

The media also bear the blame. I used to scoff at the senator's wife who wanted to put warning labels on music albums. Then I heard some of the lyrics to rap music. I will never support censorship, but there's a lot of garbage cruising through the cosmos, and young minds seem to be the preferred landing site. Arnold Schwarzenegger is unquestionably the most popular movie star among the people I teach. In *Total Recall* he puts a bullet in his wife's forehead and says, "Consider us divorced." I must have had twenty kids tell me about that scene. Then we have the mindless sitcoms, the Saturday morning cartoons, the Marvel comic books, the Sega Genesis machines . . .

Sure, kids have gotten worse, and we know why. But there's a different way to look at this. Have you considered how much harder it has become to be a teenager?

True confession time: I smoked my first marijuana cigarette when I was eighteen years old, in a dormitory as a freshman at the University of Missouri. Here's the significance—that was my first opportunity to smoke a marijuana cigarette! (Naturally, I didn't inhale.)

I passed through a drug-free high school. Oh, how the times have changed. I do a little experiment in my sophomore English classes. I ask them, "If your assignment was to bring a marijuana cigarette to class tomorrow, how many of you could do your homework?" I usually have about 90% answer affirmatively. Then I say, "Okay, how about if I change the assignment? Suppose you have to bring the cigarette to me by lunch? And you can't leave campus to get it?" The number of raised hands drops to about 50%. Invariably, there's a smart guy in class who waves his hand vigorously. "Mr. M, Mr. M," he says, "if you give me a hall pass I can go getcha one right now."

When you consider the availability of other drugs far more potent and dangerous, you realize what a minefield today's teenagers are walking through. Considering the recklessness of my own youth, I can only thank God I wasn't exposed to such lethal "pleasures" at that age.

And what about sex? Back then the boys worried about their reputations if they didn't do it, and the girls worried about theirs if they did. Nowadays that's not even an issue. Pregnancy is still a cause for concern, but after-the-fact confrontations are met with a whole new set of alternatives. I can't remember the last year I went without someone pregnant in my classroom, and I usually hear of several abortions during a school term. I shudder to think of how many I don't hear about. AIDS did not even exist when I was in school. Magic Johnson's plight has made teenagers aware that this deadly disease is not exclusively consigned to homosexuals and dope addicts. With all due respect to Magic, I doubt if there is such a thing as safe sex in high school.

But enough doomsaying. It's equally important to remember how much kids *haven't* changed. They still feel the same insecurities—it hasn't gotten any easier to ask a girl on a date; they experience the same triumphs—scoring the winning basket feels as good as it ever did; they know the same passions—first love has the same powerful impact. For all the new complexities of teenage life, the simple pleasures still exist.

You don't get into teaching because it's easy. This is the litmus test: Are you willing to fight the battle? If kids have gotten worse, then we need to make them better. It might not even matter if we win. I haven't believed I could save the world since I was a teenager; that's God's job and I'll trust Him to do it. But I'd hate to think I just stood by and watched it perish.

23
PRINCIPLES FOR PRINCIPALS
Low profile or endangered species?

One day my principal summoned me to his office. I don't like being in a principal's office—carryover from my school days, I suppose—so I went in with a certain anxiety.

"Dallin," he said, gesturing toward a chair, "we have a problem. A student's mother called me this morning to complain about a story you read yesterday in your Creative Writing class. Something about an obscene phone call. She didn't think it was appropriate for a high school class. In fact, she wanted me to read it and see what I thought."

Ah, yes. "Dial a Scare." I wrote it in a fit of envy at the big bucks Stephen King makes. My students loved that story.

"Well, sir," I began, my stomach tightening, "I guess I can see how she might take it the wrong way, since the story deals with a controversial subject. But I took special care to make sure nothing too strong was in the story; there's no bad language or anything like that. And it's real important in Creative Writing that the kids feel like no topic is taboo. I like the story; you're welcome to read it."

My principal held up his hand deprecatingly. "No offense, Dallin, but I don't have the time or inclination to read your story. I know you're a good teacher, and I have every confidence that you know how to conduct your classes. I just called you down here to make you aware of the situation. I told the woman who called that if she had a problem with a particular teacher, the first step would be to contact that teacher and talk it over. That's where things stand."

I went and called the offended mother, and while we did not reach full agreement, we did smooth things over. Most of all, I appreciated how my principal handled the situation.

It doesn't always work so well. Once a different principal summoned me to his office. "Mr. Malmgren," he began uncomfortably, "I want you to know I've sent a letter to the school board recommending you not be rehired as the journalism teacher for next year."

I stared at him in astonishment. "C-could I ask why?" I finally managed.

He shrugged. "I just don't believe you're the right person for that job."

My shock was turning to anger. "What does that mean?" I demanded. "My classroom evaluations have been good to excellent. You yourself sat in my classroom and gave me a high evaluation. In fact, you've never indicated you weren't satisfied with my work. I don't understand this."

"Oh, I think you're an excellent teacher," he admitted. "I just don't think you're right for the journalism program. Since this is your last probationary year, if you're rehired I won't be able to do anything about it later. So I have to act now."

So I went and found another teaching job, and I wrote a novel about a beleaguered high school journalism teacher. (It's called *The Ninth Issue,* and I highly recommend it.)

One principal for whom I have a great deal of respect, and one for whom I have none. Besides my own self-interest, what makes the difference?

I've asked many of my teaching colleagues what they look for in a good administrator, and I've been surprised at how varied (and sometimes contradictory) their answers have been. Still, I've heard some recurring themes. Teachers want a principal who is honest. We need to know where we stand, whether we're perceived as doing a good job or a poor one. Most of us like to face problems head on, not dance around them. And when something arises which will have an effect on our classroom, we hate being the last to know.

Teachers also want a principal who is involved. Visibility is a strong selling point. Those who hide in plush offices have probably alienated their work force. I know a principal who insists on teaching one class a day, just "to keep her hand in." So first period every day, she is a psychology teacher. The rest of the day, she's the principal. I love that attitude.

It is vital that a principal be aware of what is going on at the school. The "hear no evil, see no evil, speak no evil" principal is a relic with no place in today's educational struggle, though he is hardly an endangered species. A principal should know his school's troublemakers by sight and name, should know which cliques or crowds hang out where on the school campus, should know who is teaching and who's going through the motions, and should be doing something about it.

Finally, teachers who are teaching want to be left alone. That's why I appreciated the principal in my first example so much. He became aware of a problem in my classroom, communicated it to me, and allowed me to deal with it. Had further intervention been necessary, he could have done that without offending me. There is much to be said for a hands-off principal, especially when it comes to allowing teachers to do their jobs.

From what I've observed, the school principal who is respected and appreciated by the school's faculty is a rare breed. Part of that comes from the nature of the position. Let's face it, most people don't like their bosses. Still, I've worked in three different high schools for six different principals, and I've noticed some disturbing similarities.

1) The talent pool from which we select our school administrators seems to be heavily stocked with failed coaches and burned-out teachers. I've seen several instances where coaches, especially football coaches, have hung onto their jobs longer than their winning percentages might merit. A

school board looking for new blood in that most visible of high school positions will often offer the old man a "promotion" as a means of extricating him from the job. A 4-7 record is more acceptable for running a school than for running a football team. And many teachers find themselves so desperate to get out of the classroom that the graduate school coursework required for certification in school administration seems a negligible price to pay. Are these the best leaders we can find for our schools?

2) Most administrators' primary concern seems to be preserving their jobs—and that is a juggling act. Every principal I've ever seen seemed to have a special spectacular smile reserved exclusively for superintendents and school board members. Most principals are more concerned with the visible aspects of leadership than with what might be best for the students. The school's educational philosophy comes to mirror Andre Agassi's in the well-known camera commercial—image is everything.

3) Because of the above, administrators are inclined to put teachers at the bottom of their pecking order. We pose the least threat to them. A distraught parent can be troublesome; an angry board member is anathema; but a disgruntled teacher is merely par for the course. More pointedly, I suspect some principals take a perverse pleasure in ticking us off.

4) Most principals feel compelled to favor a traditional, don't-make-waves approach to running a school. A controversial innovation has very little chance against a time-honored tradition, regardless of potential benefit. Next to money, tradition is the popular excuse principals use for vetoing new ideas.

Despite all the above criticism, I do admire school administrators, the same way I admire toxic waste investigators, water tower painters, and undercover cops. I can't imagine why anyone would choose that line of work. A principal must be all things to all people, and he has to answer to everybody for the job he's doing. He must know when to be tough and when to be sensitive; when to butt in and when to butt out. It's an especially hard job to do well. But if he will follow one standard in his decision-making—always choose what is best for the students at his school—he will become a leader who has an impact. He'll make a difference.

 **24**

G/T, CLA, ABLE, OCS, STARS, PALs
I'll let you see my gift if I can see yours

In high school we're in the business of finding ways to get the square peg into the round hole. Mostly we just chisel at the edges, because, Lord knows, we don't want to mess with the hole.

We learn in high school that it takes all kinds to make a world. We also learn that life isn't fair, and that all men are not created equal. Thus far our primary means of dealing with the inequalities is to stamp a label on the kids, funnel them into a certain track, and let them roll along. Let's take a look at some of our labels.

G/T — Gifted and Talented   Here we have the last bastion of elitism in the public schools, but oh what a powerful fortress it is! The name says it all, and think of all the poor window-shoppers who stare enviously as the cream of the crop moves majestically through the grades.   From this select group, usually formed in the early elementary years, will come your valedictorian, salutatorian, and most of your future scholarship winners. They will be kept together in most of their classes throughout their public school years, and, believe me, no one needs to convince them they are special. In high school they will be given weighted grades for taking difficult courses, and some will graduate with grade point averages higher than 100%. The competition has grown so fierce that in my school the group has been subdivided into a G/T and an "advanced" class. Sort of like varsity and JV, I guess.

Some advice for the prospective G/T teacher: G/T is generally considered a plum teaching assignment, but beware! It does have its pitfalls. Grades mean the world to these kids, far more than highminded ideals like knowledge and understanding. Be ready to defend every answer on your test, every deduction on their essays; always have a calculator handy. And remember, hell hath no fury like a G/T parent on the prod.

CLA — Correlated Language Arts Let's move to the other end of the spectrum. CLA does not designate a specific group, but a type of class offered to a specific group. FOM (Fundamentals of Math) would be another one. These are classes designed for the "below normal"—what a tag! CLA means no college ahead, abridged versions of novels, lots of busy work, and mostly rookies and burnouts for teachers. Who goes to CLA? We move those poor pathetic students who do all their assignments and homework but make 52's on their exams. More commonly, those who want a diploma without reading a book or doing anything that resembles research gravitate to CLA. And this type of class makes a convenient hiding place for the student athlete who is more concerned about his eligibility than his education. A CLA teacher works under two mandates. The first is to drill the students on the language arts portion of the TAAS test that all Texas students must pass to graduate. The second is to keep a low failure rate.

For an experienced teacher, a CLA assignment is the kiss of death. You have fallen out of favor with the powers that be, and this is your punishment. Mostly though, the CLA assignments go to the new teachers, and when you've proven your worth you move up to regular classes and the newest teacher on the block gets your schedule. Of course, this is patently ridiculous. CLA classes are the most difficult to teach, with more discipline problems, far less motivated students, and genuine learning disabilities. All too often the beleaguered teacher's response in the face of these complexities is to worksheet them to death and send them to the office when they misbehave.

(The state of Texas in 1992 did away with all CLA, FOM, and other such courses which group together lower level students. Now these students are put into the "regular" level classes with their peers. I applaud the state's action. However, I am dismayed the state made no similar mandate moving the G/T students into the regular classes. While I recognize that homogenous grouping would certainly create more work for the classroom teacher, I believe it is the most fair and equitable method of educating our children.)

ABLE — Academic and Behavioral Learning Environment
Uh oh, we've moved into the land of "special education." This is the home of the initial labels. You've got ED (emotionally disturbed), and LD (learning disabled), which can be OHI (other health impaired), or ADHD (attention deficiency hyperactivity disorder), or scads of other things. Special ed is sort of a school's toxic waste area, a dumping ground for the most roughhewn square pegs. It's the home of catchphrases like "mainstreaming" and "skillstreaming"—phrases that sound a lot better than they look. It's the land of the paperwork avalanche; everything must be individualized, everything must be documented, and everything is the government's business. The special ed teacher deals with the abused, the neglected, the disturbed, the unwanted, the chemically unbalanced, and all the families that they come from.
Special ed teachers mostly keep to themselves; they have no time to socialize, and only another special ed teacher would understand. But let's go back to the ABLE classroom. Many teachers don't know such a classroom exists on their campus. It is "self-contained"—which sort of means that no one gets in and no one gets out. The ABLE classroom is for the ED student, but most of them are also LD or OHI or whatever. This is a pretty hardened group of young people; broken families, poverty, criminal records, and

histories of abuse are the norm. Future plans among these inmates rarely extend beyond the next weekend. What many of these kids really need is hospitalization—we're talking serious mental illness here, folks—but few of their families have any kind of comprehensive health insurance, and it's cheaper for the school districts to contain them than to pick up the medical tab.

My wife has been involved in special education for three years, the last year as a teacher. She makes about $8,000 less than I, and works about three times as hard. There is such a high turnover in Special Ed personnel that some school districts have begun offering bonuses for teaching in that field. The next time you have a chance, give a special ed teacher a hug. Or a raise.

OCS — On Campus Suspension The home of the bad. Students get assigned to OCS for being discipline problems. Fighting, creating classroom disturbances, skipping too many D-halls, cussing out a teacher—that sort of thing. OCS is a self-contained classroom in which each student is assigned a stall, with a drill sergeant type presiding over the entire motley crew. They are given assignments from their "regular" teachers to keep them busy and enable them to keep up with the class during their incarceration.

The key to an effective OCS program is that it be an unpleasant experience for the miscreants. I worked at a school where students would intentionally misbehave every so often just to take a break from the regular classroom grind. But an OCS teacher has the saddest job in a high school. You can only growl so loud, and state law prevents you from doing much more than that. One of my best friends at my school left his job as science teacher/assistant football coach and took the OCS position this past year. He doesn't know what he will do next year, but he doesn't want to be back in OCS. "If I'm going to work with trash," he says, "I'm at least going to get paid like a garbage collector."

So far I've focused on special students programs which are not, in my opinion, doing a very effective job of shaping our square pegs.

I feel a little guilty saying that, because I know a number of teachers (my wife, for instance) in these programs who are pouring out their lives for the sake of their students. I don't have any concrete answers for meeting the special needs of students myself. I am pleased to see that many school districts are coming up with new, innovative programs to try and meet some of the challenges these students present. My district has introduced two programs in the past three years that are worth mentioning:

STARS—Strategies with Technology and Affective and Remedial Support The wave of the future. This is something new on our campus, funded by a government grant (the kiss of death?). I just hope the funding doesn't run out before we see what the program can do, because the possible benefits are great. Those students deemed "at-risk" (potential dropouts) are selected for the program. During their ninth and tenth grade years they are provided individualized instruction through the use of computer technology, small group counseling, and a link with the community through a mentor program. During their junior and senior years the students should be able to secure part-time work or internships in local businesses with the help of their mentors. Parental involvement is stressed, and the teachers who run the STARS program spend a good deal of their time making home visits and helping parents help their kids. Sounds wonderful, doesn't it? I've talked with a number of students who are involved in the program, and I've heard quite often that STARS is the only thing that's keeping their heads above water, educationwise. On the other hand, I've had one student from the STARS program in my sophomore English class. He flunked the semester with a 58%. Can a leopard change his spots? Of course, the jury is still out on this sort of thing. But we have to do something to address the problem of high school dropouts, and this is innovative. I am interested.

PALs — Peer Assistance Leadership We just started this program this year, so it's impossible to judge its effectiveness.

Similar to the cooperative learning movement, the foundational idea is that of students helping students. Juniors and seniors are nominated by teachers to serve as PALs. These PALs are trained to work as peer helpers with younger students either on their campus or with students on the junior high, middle school, and elementary school campuses. The PALs do every thing from providing a listening ear to helping with academics to offering encouragement in dealing with drug, family, or attendance problems. Troubled students are referred to PALs by teachers, friends, or even themselves. No one is forced to participate.

There are two really fine ideas that underpin this program. It develops a sense of social responsibility in those young people who participate as PALs. They are coming face-to-face with real problems in the community, and they are being asked to play a role in doing something about them. We are also recognizing that students have far greater access to one another's lives than we do. A student who would not be caught dead opening up to a teacher or counselor can find it quite easy to talk candidly with one of his peers. Often, they are also more willing to listen to advice. Again, it's too early for me to tell how effective PALs will be. But it seems like a step in the right direction.

I don't know how to solve the square pegs/round hole quandary that our school systems face. Certainly, we must make every effort to meet the special needs of each student that we attempt to educate. I don't think that anyone involved in any of the above programs would insist that we are doing that with great effectiveness. But in a very real sense, every single student comes to us with special needs, and the task we face is impossible. I can't offer any solutions, other than that we perhaps shift our focus on where the responsibility for an education lies.

I wrote a novel once about a high school foreign exchange student. In preparation for writing the book, I interviewed dozens of students from other countries and asked them about their impressions of American education. I came away with one overriding observation: In other countries an education is considered a privilege, and the burden of acquiring an education is placed upon the student, not the teacher. The foreign exchange students were astounded at how many worksheets, homework grades, daily grades, quizzes, etc., that an American teacher recorded in his gradebook. In their countries you needed to pass the exam to show you had mastered the material in order to advance. They all seemed to have a much greater grasp of one simple truism—education is the key to success. They felt responsible to learn. I wish more of my students felt that way.

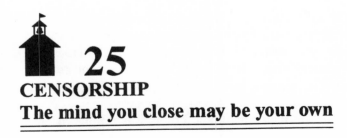

25
CENSORSHIP
The mind you close may be your own

I read the news today. Oh boy. They're still at it. Someone in (fill in the blank) freaked out upon learning *The Grapes of Wrath* ends with an old man sucking milk from a young woman's breast. Someone in (fill in the blank) hit the roof when he learned what kind of jokes Juliet's nurse was making in *Romeo and Juliet*. Parents in (fill in the blank) stormed the school board when their son told them Chaucer wrote a story in which a lady sticks her rear out the window to be kissed.

Then there was the history teacher in (fill in the blank) who got in trouble for questioning the legitimacy of America's intervention in Iraq. Or the government teacher in (fill in the blank) who was suspended for calling flag burning an appropriate form of political expression. Or the journalism teacher in (fill in the blank) who lost her job for okaying an article about teenage pregnancy.

The late Supreme Court justice William O. Douglas wrote: " . . . the restriction of free thought and free speech is the most dangerous of all subversions." Well, there's a lot of subversives running around out there these days.

Who are these people? I used to carry around this stereotype of guys driving pickup trucks with red necks and beer cans in coozies, whose only solutions to a problem involved a shotgun or a match.

In fact, we're more likely to find them sitting next to us in a church pew, neatly dressed and fervently concerned about their child's education. They more than likely wish they could afford to home-school their child or have him in a private religious school, but they are determined to make the best of a bad situation. They see their protests as a form of Christian service or ministry.

While I admire their conviction, I think it is misplaced. My fundamental difference with these people is that they are undermining my work. How can I encourage their children to think (my most basic goal) when they are spouting the notion that ideas are dangerous? I am a Christian man, but I want my children to be able to look evil in the face, recognize it for what it is, and turn away from it. I do not want them to be ignorant of it, or unaware of its existence. The real world would crush them.

But there is another type of subversive far more insidious than the so-called Bible thumper. That is the principal whose bottom line is Don't Make Waves, or the teacher whose modus operandi is We've Always Done It This Way, or the board member whose first objection is No One Else Is Trying That. These people pose the greater threat to free thought and free speech.

Because the battle against censorship is two-fold. Certainly we have to stand up for our right to teach ideas. But that is not enough. We also have to make our students be willing to think. Now there's a challenge.

Every year on the first day of school I give my students a little pep talk on the innate joys of studying English and especially literature. "Literature is just people writing about life," I explain, "and everybody knows about life because everybody has one. When we read, we find out what someone else has learned about life. Besides, it's fun." One year I noticed a boy in the front row shaking his head. Danny Togo was a New Waver, and somehow he was able to manipulate his hair so it stood straight up from his skull, almost six inches. When a kid like that shakes his head, you can't help but notice. It's like having a field of wheat in the classroom. Anyway, I asked him, "What's the matter, Danny, don't you think you can study literature and have fun at the same time?" "No, I don't," he said stonily. "Why not?" I asked. "Because you have to think when you read."

He had me there. You do have to think when you read. If you don't, you keep going back to the same place.

Now, what in the name of Nintendo has taught these youngsters that you have to disengage your brain in order to enjoy yourself?

I guess some of the responsibility for the difficulty we have getting students to think lies with the teachers. Reading, like writing, is basically a creative act, because it connects the reader with his imagination. When you remove the creativity, you take most of the fun out of it. Unfortunately, we do that all the time, by telling them what they have to read, what they should think about what they just read, and what they must do as a result of having read it.

So what should teachers do? I'm certainly not an advocate of anarchy in the classroom, but I do think most teachers could be less concerned with having the students learn it *their* way, and more concerned with just letting them learn it. We need teachers who are innovators, risk takers. Too many teachers will settle for bored quietude in the classroom, and for some the idea of independent thinking is quite intimidating. You see, if a student can analyze a math problem, he or she can also analyze how well you're doing at teaching it.

Of course you're taking chances when you encourage them to think. A few years ago I came up with a new idea in my creative writing class. We invented the Dead Philosophers Society (borrowing shamelessly from a popular film). About once a month we selected a list of topics to discuss, took a night to mull them over, then sat in a circle and exchanged our ideas. We talked about love and death, about success and education, about the environment and the future, about sex and date rape and homosexuality and romance and premarital sex and dating. (As you can see, the conversation drifted in a certain direction.)

At one of our DPS meetings, one of the topics was the Berlin

Wall. A boy named Shawn chose to talk about that. Shawn had had some legal problems, and he'd also spent time in a mental hospital. Shawn had very strong feelings about the Berlin Wall. "I want to tell you, I've spent time in jail," he said. "I know what it's like when someone can tell you where you can and can't go. You can't imagine the sound of bars closing you in. And I'm telling you, when you don't have your freedom, I don't give a fuck who you are, you don't have anything."

The class, as you can imagine, fell completely silent, partly because they saw the tears in Shawn's eyes and recognized the real emotion in his voice, and partly because they had never heard the F word in a classroom before. They all looked at me.

I thanked Shawn for his opinion, agreed that there was nothing so valuable as freedom (another F word), and went on to the next person in the circle. Of course, if my principal had walked by at that time . . .

When I think of intellectual freedom as it pertains to high school, I don't see us merely as defenders of a sacred right. We have to do that, certainly. We must stand up every time the freedom to think is threatened, whether in the school library or the school newspaper or the school classroom. But we're more than defenders—we're liberators. We have to be, because there are a lot of Danny Togos in the world, kids who truly believe you can't think and have fun at the same time. And those kids are in intellectual shackles.

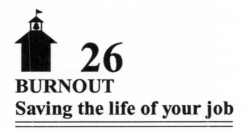

26
BURNOUT
Saving the life of your job

You read about it in newspapers and educational journals. You cannot walk into a faculty lounge without observing some of its scarred victims. You can't get through a day without suspecting you've begun to contract the symptoms. The question is not *if* you will get it but *when*. And how bad. Burnout in the teaching profession is as inevitable as zeros in the gradebook.

Or do you already have it? Until now the only measuring stick we've had to determine how burned out we really are is direct comparison with our colleagues around us. This can engender a false sense of security, since some of those around us teach with the passion of a lump of used charcoal. Therefore, as a public service I've devised the Ultimate Teacher Burnout Test. The results are as scientific as the standardized test scores your school district foists upon the community every year.

1) Do you refuse to take work home?

2) Do you leave the campus within ten minutes after the last bell?

3) Do you make it a practice never to volunteer for anything?

4) Is your faculty lounge conversation marked by a stream of cynical remarks about education and young people? -OR-

5) Do you make it a point never to converse about anything related to your job?

6) Do you play the lottery and vacation in Las Vegas?

7) Do you hate your principal with psychopathic intensity?

8) Have you used the same exact lesson plans for more than two years?

9) Do you frequently forget the names of the people in your classroom?

10) Do you go through Mondays without smiling?

11) Do you have no hope for the future of mankind?

12) Do Real Life Teachers avoid you?

—If you answered "yes" to more than nine of the questions, you have reached the mental state of an igneous rock. Get a job in a convenience store (on the night shift).

—If you answered "yes" on seven to nine questions, you are hovering on the level of a campfire around midnight. Look for firewood, the coyotes are howling.

—If you answered "yes" on four to six questions, put the steaks on right away. I hope you like your meat rare.

—If you answered "yes" on one to three questions, you're in the prime of your career. Enjoy it.

—If you had no "yesses," go work for Walt Disney. Teaching has no room for fools.

The first mistake would be to quickly condemn your clearly identifiable burned-out colleagues. No one comes into the profession burned out, and most enter with high-minded ideals. That was as true ten, fifteen, or twenty years ago as it is today. Every hollow shell you observe going through the motions at the front of the classroom could have once been an excellent teacher. If they have been brought down, it has been by the rigors of the job.

For the rigors are inestimable. Stress is a way of life for a teacher. He faces the stress of performing, of report cards and evaluations, of antagonistic students, of mountains of paperwork, of broken down copying machines, of limited budgets, of additional duties unrelated to teaching but still part of the job. Is it any wonder some of us respond like kindling?

Sympathies notwithstanding, a truth must not be overlooked. **Burnout is fatal.** It cannot be left untreated. It is not a phase or a mood, and it will not just go away. Burnout is a chronic disease, and a deadly one, eating away at you twenty-four hours a day, sapping all joy from your life, receding in the summer but returning fullblown in the fall. Burnout makes you bored and boring. Worse yet, it is infectious. You become a carrier, passing it on to your students, who are highly susceptible and who carry it with them to other classrooms, until it becomes an epidemic capable of devastating an entire school. You can tell just by walking into some buildings.

Happily, it doesn't have to be this way. There's a simple cure for burnout. It's called change. Radical cases demand radical therapy. Get out. Switch careers. Find a new job. You owe it to yourself, and, more importantly, you owe it to your students. However, most cases of burnout are not so advanced and require less drastic measures. The key is still change. Teach a different grade or a different subject. To teach something new, you must learn something new. Most teachers are hesitant to change teaching assignments because such a change almost always means added work. True, but remember that the path of least resistance leads downward. Change is rarely easy, but it's usually healthy.

I know of a man who quit teaching after seventeen years. When he left, he'd have scored a perfect yes on the Ultimate Teacher Burnout Test. He went out and sold kitchen tile or something for a year, and then he came back. Last year he won the Teacher of the Year award in his school district. Change works.

If a change in your teaching assignment is not possible or

seems too stressful, there are other changes you can make. Teach differently. Mix it up. Take your class outside under a tree and read to them. Try new things. Make a vow to learn something new about one of your students every day. Change your style, dress funny, switch classrooms, get a new conference period, park in a different spot, exercise at lunchtime, perm your hair, tell jokes, whatever it takes. Change works.

The greatest compliment I have ever received came from a burned-out teacher. Mr. Kern taught next door to me with only a partition dividing us. Neither one of us much liked the other. On the last day of school of my last year there (I was moving to Texas), Mr. Kern stopped me in the hallway.

"You know, Malmgren, I have to thank you," he said.

"For what?" I asked in surprise.

"Well, with your class as noisy as it is, and us right next to each other, I've had to listen to you a lot. And you taught me something. No, actually you made me remember something."

"What's that?" I asked cautiously.

"You reminded me how important it is to really enjoy the kids. I'd forgotten that, and it makes all the difference. I want to thank you for it." He shook my hand.

I like to think Mr. Kern taught better the next year. I know I did.

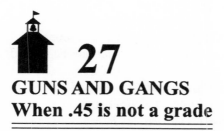

27
GUNS AND GANGS
When .45 is not a grade

The scariest thing that ever happened to me in the classroom occurred in a creative writing class. In reference to nothing that was going on in the class discussion, Charles raised his hand and said, "You know, Mr. Malmgren, it would be super easy for me to hide a gun in my bookbag and just pull it out in the middle of this class and open fire."

A little about Charles: I had first taught him in sophomore English two years earlier. He failed the second semester, though he was brighter than most in that class. He didn't do a research paper, as I recall. Charles was a tormented soul. His real mother committed suicide when he was four or five, and I'm told he was the one who discovered the body. In high school Charles was handsome, popular, and feared. In his sophomore year he was walking the edge. In the classroom I saw flashes of unfocused anger, a clear disregard for authority or morality, and a cruel cunning.

By his senior year he'd crossed over. He was on probation for masterminding a burglary ring, composed mostly of some of the better athletes from our school. One night at a party he held a knife to a pretty cheerleader's throat because she had somehow made him jealous. He had done two stretches, one rather lengthy, in a local mental hospital. Now he was back in school.

Naturally, I was nonplussed by his comment. "Boy, Charles, that's really a pleasant thought to have rolling around in your head," I said, trying to play it off. Charles grinned. Sometimes he looked like Jack Nicholson when he smiled. After class I went and found an assistant principal and told him what Charles had said. He seemed concerned, but he really didn't know what to do about it. He told me he would talk to Charles and call his father. Later in the day I saw Charles. Our school has an open mall area in the middle of it, with a stairway that leads up to the second floor. At the top of the stairs you can look across the mall to the hallway on the other side. I saw him across the way, and he smiled again, and raised his hand in the shape of a gun, and made a silent "pow" with his mouth, and blew the smoke from the top of his finger. Scared hell out of me.

I didn't sleep too well that night, and I gave some serious thought toward calling in sick the next day. When Charles came into creative writing class, I eyed his bookbag warily. He walked up to my desk and told me he was "supposed" to say he was sorry about what he said, and that he was just "joking around." I said I was glad. Then he added if he was going to shoot a teacher, it wouldn't be me, it would be his Spanish teacher. And that was the end of it.

Doesn't that make you feel better? If mine were an isolated incident, it wouldn't be a cause for much concern, but I suspect every teacher with a few years' experience has a similar story to tell, many with a more unhappy ending.

This year the gangs arrived at our safe, suburban school. Oh, we've heard about gang activities for the past few years, with words like "wannabes" and "posers" bandied about. But now they are here, like the killer bees. In October a boy named Eddie who went to our school (my wife had him in her Emotionally Disturbed class) was shot in front of a convenience store in our district. Four boys from a rival gang that go to school in the district bordering ours participated in the "driveby." Eddie lost a portion of his brain as a result of the shooting, and he'll spend the rest of his life in a hospital bed. Our school district responded with an inservice on "gang awareness." We were given a bunch of handouts. I showed them to a few kids in my sophomore English class who are on the periphery of gang activity (at least). They had a good laugh over the information we were given. We are not exactly way ahead of these people.

Last semester a student came up to my desk with something he wanted to show me. It was a computer printout, about twenty pages, full of information about how to make explosives, incendiary devices, and other destructive implements out of materials you could purchase in any local hardware store at very little cost. All of the instructions were couched in radical, anarchical, hip hop slang. I asked the student where he got it.

"My friend got it off his computer. He just had his modem hooked up to some bulletin board or something. Pretty cool, huh?"

"What do you want it for?"

"I don't know. It's just good to have. I'm acquiring an education."

"I see."

"Can I have it back?"

"No." (This from a man who has given a number of speeches decrying censorship.)

It's getting scary out there, folks. And I don't just mean the high schools. Today in the faculty lounge one of the teachers was confessing with a giggle that her son (now a freshman) had been kicked off the school bus when he was in kindergarten.

"What did he do?" I asked.

"I can't even remember," she said. "I think he stood up while the bus was moving."

"That's nothing," another teacher said. "My daughter had one of her kindergarten students get kicked off the bus last week. But that was for pulling a knife on the bus."

So maybe it's just my school district? I don't think so. I saw a piece on the national news about a week ago where the focus was on the threat of violence in schools, which had become so serious in districts in California and New Jersey that they were using metal detectors at the school entrances. We haven't even considered that yet. And around a year ago I read about a boy in Kentucky who read Stephen King's story "Rage" (about a boy who kills his teacher and then holds his class hostage), and decided to try it out in his classroom. One dead teacher.

I don't believe it is possible to teach effectively when one of your main concerns is personal safety. Nor is it possible to learn. Violence in the schools is not an issue that needs to be addressed; it's a reality that demands immediate, concerted action. School officials have to be given the authority to do whatever it takes to make our schools a safe place again.

In the wake of the gang activity that has cropped up in our community and our schools, the school district has adopted a policy called "zero tolerance." The idea is that no trace of gang activity will be tolerated, and that any student participating in such activity will be summarily removed from the school. It remains to be seen how effective this program will be in dealing with the problems that confront us, but I do like the concept.

And I do see some positive signs. For the past several years, we've had an increase in the number of physical fights that have broken out between students at our high school. A fight brings out the absolute worst in mass adolescent behavior. A huge crowd encircles the combatants, no effort is made to intervene, and every punch, scratch, or bite is greeted with enormous approval from the audience. (The crowd really gets enthusiastic when the combatants are girls.) A teacher or other person in authority has to fight his way through that mob and attempt to separate the antagonists amidst cries of "Let them fight!" and "Stay out of it!" and "Hit the teacher!" Some teachers have told me they no longer will do anything to break up a fight in progress; others have said they just wait to step in until there is a clear winner. Well, the last fight I saw at our school ended with both participants being handcuffed and dragged out to waiting patrol cars while the mob watched in stunned silence. That happened two months ago, and I don't remember a fight since.

Good job, administration.

But more can be done. My biggest complaint is with the lack of information circulated to us teachers, who are really on the front lines of this battlefield. Last year at least two students were caught bringing weapons into the school building. I never found out who those two students were. That's something I'd like to know. I'd also like to know which of the students I teach are on probation, and for what; which ones have histories of mental illness; which ones blew up in another teacher's classroom the previous day. Oh, I suppose I get a lot of this information as it is, but most of it comes from students I talk with, not the most reliable source.

When I worked in the mental hospital, we had chart rounds at every change of shift before we went out on the ward. We'd review any problem situations that might be anticipated. Or remember how they always had roll call at the beginning of that great cop show, "Hill Street Blues"? I wouldn't mind having something like that at school. I'd like to know who just got put in OCS (On Campus Suspension) and why, why the cops were on campus yesterday, what the story was behind the bomb threat, etc. Loneliness is a horrible feeling in the middle of a war.

You can blame it on the lack of gun control or drug abuse or the breakdown of family values or a million other things, but the days of feeling safe in your school seem to be over. You see, Charles was right. It is super easy for any kid, whether a fledgling gang member wanting to prove his courage or a crazed psycho battling unseen demons, to bring a gun into a school. Chances are, there's nothing you can do to prevent it, and little you can do to anticipate it.

They are out there, I promise. I sponsor the school's literary magazine at my high school, and the following was submitted anonymously to me for consideration of publication. I reproduce it here with all its original atrocities:

He aimed his gun recklessly at the other, slowly pulled back the trigger and rubbed his index finger smoothly over thee semmingly endless trigger. "I have a wife and two kids" the

other man screamed at him, but the man in the trenchcoat just laughed and shoved the gun deep into his throat, touching his tosils causing him to vomit tand gag extracting his last meal which appeared to be chicken noodle soup all over the man in the trenchcoat's boots and .357 nickel-plated revvolver. He fired once blowing the rear half of his head off instantaneously. The man in black slowly wiped off his gun, reholstered it, then stared at his latest kill. If another person was around to look deep into the man in black's eyes he could see a change, a transformation of san to insane. I love insane people so I write about them. The man in black rolled back his eyes, threw back his head and began to laugh, he began to laugh out of control and started kicking the dead man where his head was blown apart. He finally stopped and walked away far away. Many thoughts raced through his mind as he walked. Why do I have this disease??? Why do I write about these things that I wish I could do to every single person that has ever bothered me??? If I had that nickel-plated .357 magnum and could have possession of that large beautiful piece of art, I would, And I would start with you you you you fuck you I will kill you you geletin ass fuck. . . .When I attain my agehood of 21 I will I will I will Fuck you you shit, stink. You may read of me, but you may not. . .
A sick mind will be captured, I am sick. . . But I am a sick-minded intelligent motherfucker

Just think—someone is expected to teach that young mind how to write. Any volunteers?

28
FARTHER ALONG
Year-'round school and other notions

I am feeling depressed. *Parade* magazine's annual "What People Earn" issue just came out. A tailor in Edmond, Oklahoma, makes $34,000. A telephone technician in Lincoln, Nebraska, makes $35,000. A tavern owner in Columbus, Ohio, makes $40,000. Stephen King makes $15 million, for God's sake.

My salary for the 1992-93 school year, after twelve years of teaching and before taxes, was $29,873.33. My wife, in her second year of teaching, made $21,492.00.

Ten years after the landmark study of the American educational system, "A Nation at Risk", declared that the system was, in fact, in shambles, the consensus of opinion remains the same—the system is still in shambles, and the nation is still at risk. The first point I want to make about the future of public education in America is that the system will not be improved without more money. That is not self-interest; it is simple fact.

That fact is readily apparent to anyone who works in a school. The teacher across the hall from me turned in her resignation last month. She was a brilliant teacher. She is going to work in a travel agency. She'll make a comparable salary, she'll spend forty hours per week at her job, and she won't take any work home with her. As she explains it, "I'll have a life."

I wish that somehow the general public could be forced to observe the difference between what happens in a classroom led by an energetic, vibrant, committed teacher and one led by a drone. I guarantee the kids know the difference. The topnotch students at our school scoff at the idea of becoming teachers. They observe firsthand how hard it is, and they're well aware of the salary range. Quality education won't happen without quality educators, and you cannot attract them (or keep them) without making it worth their while.

The economic issues extend far beyond teacher salaries, though. My school district recently put together something called the Strategic Planning Committee. A group of volunteers from within the administration, the different faculties, and the community at large met for several days with the purpose of mapping out a ten-year plan for our district. The group identified five areas which needed to be addressed: facilities, technology, staff, innovative programs, and community involvement. Next, action teams were assembled to develop plans for each specific area. The action teams were instructed to dream, i.e., to think in terms of what could be done within their area to enhance the educational opportunities for all the people in the district, instead of worrying about how to get the money to do them.

Oh, what marvelous ideas we generated! The Facilities committee foresaw a new elementary school with an Early Childhood Center, two new intermediate schools (our district is growing rapidly), a fine arts center at the high school, and all kinds of renovations on existing buildings.

Our Technology committee hoped for computer availability at every grade level, computer training for every teacher, computer experts on every campus to troubleshoot problem areas, satellite technology, interactive software, and other things I didn't even understand.

Our Staff committee proposed salaries competitive with the wealthiest districts in the area, a recruitment program designed to lure the best and the brightest graduating from schools of education, health care for all district personnel, and a diverse selection of opportunities for professional growth and development.

Our Innovative Programs committee (I served on that one) proposed the construction of an alternative school, designed to provide at-risk students and drop-outs the opportunity to complete their diplomas in a manner (i.e., flexible scheduling, self-paced curriculum) conducive to their particular needs. We wanted to do away with letter/number grades on the elementary level. We favored instituting a voluntary year-round school program at one of our elementary schools, and we wanted to create a Training Academy where administrators could become more aware of the needs of staff and students and the availability of programs designed to meet those needs.

Enough. I won't even mention the great ideas the Community Involvement committee came up with. Ah, what a wish list! But everything I've mentioned would have a beneficial effect on our educational community, and some of the ideas, properly implemented, would work miracles. The Strategic Planning Committee was of one mind in its primary goal—seeking what's best for our children.

Alas, everything mentioned above also costs money. To fund even some of the programs that the Strategic Planning Committee would like to institute, the taxpayers of our community are going to have to undergo a major transformation in the priority they give to public education.

There's another aspect of the economic issue that I haven't even mentioned: fairness. If one school district spends $6,000 per pupil to educate its children, and another spends $2,500 per pupil, which kids are likely to learn more? The Texas legislature is wrestling with the equal funding issue as I write this, and many other states are engaged in similar struggles. Our legislature is under a court order to establish a more equitable method of funding before the next school year begins, or the next school year will not begin. Predictably, the people in Austin have done a pretty good job of mucking it up so far. But no one should be fooled by this. If we cannot provide quality education for all the children in our nation, then the words ". . . with liberty and justice for all . . ." are a joke.

Of course, there are other factors than purely economic ones to consider in examining what lies ahead for public education. It's just very difficult to sort through some of them. Education has always been very susceptible to trends and fads. In the past twenty years we have weathered mini-courses, team teaching, several revivals of the "back to the basics" movement, assertive discipline, and numerous other approaches to providing instruction. In fact, it's always kind of interesting to go to the first inservice training session of the year and find out what the latest catchphrase is going to be. Here are some of the current ones making the rounds or looming on the horizon:

Site-based management — The idea is to return more of the power of decision-making in terms of how a school functions and is run to the people who are most involved in running it. We teachers are promised we will have a larger voice in what happens at our schools. Sounds good to me, but I'll believe it when I see it.

Cooperative learning — The teacher becomes more of a facilitator, and the students are put into smaller groups or teams, with the responsibility of teaching one another. Teams compete with one another to demonstrate content mastery. I've tried this one with mixed results. While the students do respond better to a peer than a teacher, you have to guard against the "smart" kids doing all the work for the team while the others sit back and visit.

Block scheduling — Restructuring the high school schedule to look more like a college one. Your English class might meet for an hour and forty minutes three times a week instead of for one hour everyday. It's supposed to allow more time devoted to instruction and less to paperwork, a greater variety of electives, and a more relaxed atmosphere.

The voucher system — This is the one the politicians like. (That should tell us something right away.) Parents are issued vouchers and can choose themselves where to send their children to school. Those schools which collect the most vouchers will thrive, and those which lose vouchers will wither and die. Capitalism at work. Sounds to me like a tremendous waste of existing resources. Also sounds like the public relations office will become the most important room in the school building.

Year-round schools — As precious as my summers are to me, this seems like a sound concept. The traditional school schedule was designed to accommodate an agrarian society. We no longer fit that description. Year-round schools should make more efficient use of existing facilities, provide more flexibility in scheduling, and enhance retention of learning. A modest prediction: year-round schools will be the rule and not the exception by the year 2000.

I'm sure I've missed some trends and developments, but that gives you a preview. This much I know—we, as teachers, cannot be resistant to change. The *traditional* public school system is no longer working because the *traditional* public it served has disappeared. The high school drop-out rate in Texas is almost 33 percent. We can blame the young punks we see hanging out on the street corner when we drive past, or we can recognize that we're not meeting the needs of a significant portion of our clientele. We have to change.

And change costs money. When I started out as a teacher and my wife stayed home to raise our children, we were very poor. In grocery stores, we bought the items with generic labels. We bought the "Reduced for Quick Sale" meats. Out of necessity, we managed to forget that the stuff that costs more tastes better. But it does. Just because it's a cliché doesn't mean it's not true—you get what you pay for.

29
TO TEACH OR NOT TO TEACH
Advice to the uninitiated

I've discovered a similarity between being a teacher and being a writer. It seems that everybody and his cousin has thought, at one time or another, about being one or the other. Do you suppose it's because they both appear to be fairly easy jobs from the outside looking in? Ha!

All teachers field inquiries from those who are considering the career. In high school many of the questions come from those in our classrooms, especially juniors and seniors who have begun to contemplate their career options. What's it like? Do you enjoy it? Do you think I could do it? Is the pay really as bad as they say?

Hard. Mostly. Maybe. Yes.

Actually, I've developed a stock response for everyone who shows an interest in the profession. First I ask them what grade or level they want to teach. Then I ask them if they like the people at that level. Because if you don't like eight year olds, don't teach second grade, and if you don't like teenagers, stay out of secondary schools. If you don't like young people, don't teach. And if you're not sure, find out before you commit a college education to it.

Seems obvious? You'd be amazed at how many teachers have ignored that simple guideline. I always feel a creepy chill run up my back when I'm talking with a teacher who clearly hates his students.

What a sad life!

Now, I do not mean that you have to like *all* of your students. (You won't, I promise.) But you need to have an affinity for the age group you work with. A teacher friend of mine complained the other day that her sophomores showed no appreciation for the extra time and effort she spent helping them learn geometry. I told her it comes with the territory. Our own teenage years were probably the most self-centered time of our lives. Why should theirs be different?

Ah, but teachers (and would-be teachers) need structure. Perhaps my litmus test is too simplistic? Okay, let's get analytical. Let's get compulsive. (Good trait for a teacher, though it could lead to insanity.) Let's make a list.

The Plusses	The Minuses
1) You get summers off.	1) You are not well paid.
2) Your work is meaningful.	2) You will be discouraged.
3) You are in control.	3) You're surrounded by bureaucracy
4) There are magic moments.	4) You'll lose more than you win.
5) It gets better as years go by.	5) The first year is a killer.
6) Some kids look up to you.	6) The community won't respect you.
7) It allows time for your family.	7) You'll feel guilty when you're not doing schoolwork.
8) You affect the future.	8) The future will look dismal.
9) There's no corporate ladder.	9) It's a dead-end job.
10) You have good working hours.	10) The work never ends.

I don't think I've painted a very rosy picture—that's good, it's not a rosy job. The profession needs people who like to face challenges. Not that I want to talk anyone out of teaching—just the opposite, in fact. One of the thrills of my career came in 1988 when I gave a speech at the National Council of Teachers of English in St. Louis. I was browsing through the exhibits and bumped into little Cathy Meyer. Cathy had been in my English III class four years earlier. I hadn't seen her since I moved to Texas.

"What are you doing at NCTE?" I asked after hugging her.

"I just finished up my student teaching," she said proudly, "and I got a job. I'll start teaching junior high English in January."

A disciple! I almost burst with pride. I could remember exactly where she had sat in my classroom, and things she would ask, and her vitality as a student. Now she'd be out there raising up more disciples. It was a semireligious experience.

However, there are two sides to that. I like to ask my teaching colleagues if they would advise their own children to become teachers. I haven't kept an exact count, but, believe me, the noes overwhelmingly outnumber the yeses. It's analogous to the old test for exposing someone's true level of prejudice: Would you want your sister to marry one?

I'm inclined to think there are more teachers who have a sense of regret about entering the profession than those who have a sense of fulfillment. Be warned, but don't be scared off.

You see, I've discovered another similarity between being a teacher and being a writer. In both cases, we don't get to see most of the good that we do. We want desperately to affect people's lives, to make a difference. But writers seldom see the effect of their words, and most of our students pass through our classroom and leave us wondering if we've influenced them at all.

I learned a while back that just because we don't see the results of our actions doesn't mean they don't have any. My wife had just given birth to our third child, Zachary, at Barnes Hospital in St. Louis. I taught in Ste. Genevieve, sixty miles down the river, and everyday after I school I would drive up to visit my wife and new son. One day when I came up, I had to make sure I went back to Ste. Genevieve right after the visit because my school was having Parents' Night that evening. (You don't ever miss Parents' Night.)

After the visit I went out to the Barnes Hospital parking lot and got in my car. It wouldn't start. So I got out and lifted the hood and stared at the engine. An older man was walking through the parking lot, and he asked me what the problem was. I told him I had no idea. So he started tinkering around, and after about twenty minutes he told me to get in and give it a try. My car started right up. Now, while he was tinkering around, I had looked in my wallet and discovered that I only had three dollars.

So I said to him, "Boy, I really appreciate your help. I only have three bucks on me, but you're welcome to it."

He held up his hand. "I don't want your money," he said. "But there is something you can do for me. The next time you have a chance to do something good for someone else, you make sure you do it."

I thought that was really cool, and I assured him I would do that. Then I got in my car and left. You can get from Barnes Hospital to the highway quicker if you take a shortcut through Forest Park. I don't know what it's like now, but back then Forest Park had a "reputation." You weren't supposed to go in there after dark.

But it was only dusk, and I was in a hurry. I came to a fourway stop in the park, and a man was standing there trying to flag down a car. He was a big man, and his clothes were kind of ragged. With some hesitancy I rolled down my window as I pulled up to him.

"I'm so glad you stopped," he said gratefully. "I ran out of gas, and I need a few bucks just so I can get back to East St. Louis. Do you think you could help me out?" He pointed to his car pulled over on the side of the road.

I had three dollars in my wallet. I pulled them out and handed them to him.

"Oh, man, thanks a lot," he said. "This is great. Listen, just let me write down your name and address, and I'll send the money back to you as soon as I get home."

I held up my hand. "I don't want your money," I said, "but there is something you can do for me. . . ."

Of course, the man in the parking lot never knew about the man in the park. And you won't know what happens to the kid in the third row who smiles when Scout gives Boo Radley her arm and walks him home. But every time you get one of them to open a book, every time you get one of them to think about something a bit differently, every time you get one of them to try and express himself, you're doing good.

30
RANDOM NOTES
Opinions in search of an essay

As I finish up this collection of essays, I'm left with a number of subjects about which I have strong feelings, but which I cannot develop into full blown essays (or perhaps I'm too tired). However, I've always been one to voice my opinions, and I've never minded leaving anywhere after having the last word, so I'll try a scattershot approach:

No Pass/No Play In Texas they passed an edict in 1984 (and renewed it in '93) that a student who failed a subject (a 70% is passing) for a six weeks' grading period would be ineligible to participate in extracurricular activities for the next six weeks. We've had a lot of controversy about it ever since. Here is one voice in favor of the ruling. As tennis coach I have lost vital players at rather crucial times in the season, but I still think the benefits of No Pass/No Play far outweigh the negatives. Truth is, students try harder in the classroom for the simple reason that they want to stay eligible. Since motivation is one of the greatest difficulties in the classroom today, I'd hate to see us give up an effective tool. No Pass/No Play also provides a venue for teachers and coaches to work together to see that a student/athlete keeps his priorities right during the season.

Now if we could only do something about the offseason.

Failure rates I know I've talked about this in previous essays, but things are getting out of hand. This year our school came up with the "reteach, retest" policy. This means that if a student makes less than a 70% on a test in my class, I am responsible for reteaching the material and retesting the student. Clearly, this is ridiculous. It no longer matters if the student did the work in my class, or listened, or studied, or even came to class—I am being held responsible for the failing grade. I have heard of teacher accountability, but we're carrying it to absurd lengths. My principal warns me that it is going to get worse. Pretty soon we are going to be expected to come up with IEP's (Individualized Education Plans) for any student who makes a failing grade in any class, the way we do now for special education students. Any teacher in America could tell you the real reason failure rates are going up: students are doing less and less of the work required. In reality, there have been two primary results of the new "reteach, retest" policy. Teachers get around it by scheduling the "reteach, retest" time during lunch or after school. Most of the failing students never show up, and the teacher has fulfilled the obligation of offering it. The second result is far more insidious. Feeling the pressure from above to lower failure rates, teachers are watering down the material to be tested over, making tests easier, and teaching specifically to those tests. We end up with a lower failure rate without any corollary increase in the students' skills. There has to be a better way.

Attendance How can I teach you if you're not here? The number one cause of failure in my class is absenteeism, and there isn't a close second. I had a girl on my roster for the entire first semester who came to my class a total of two times. And one of those times she went to the bathroom and didn't come back! The attendance policy at my school is even screwier than the "reteach, retest" policy. We just mark it down on a slip if a student is absent. If they're there, they're there. When a student returns they don't need any readmit slip. After nine absences in a semester, the student automatically fails a class—unless she can get a doctor's note excusing some of the absences . . . or she can present some extenuating circumstances to the principal . . . or she can make up some of the time missed by attending a special Saturday Attendance School. Nine days off out of ninety. Are there any employers out there who will buy that? Compounding the problem, most students seem to think that if they were absent, the class didn't do anything. Assignments do not get made up, and I frequently hear when I pass out a test, "Hey, I wasn't here for this." Then I get to reteach and retest them, only they're usually absent for that, too.

Teachers vs. Parents vs. Kids I used to blame the parents for their kids' absenteeism and missing assignments and poor classroom behavior, too. I realize now that was as wrong as their blaming me. This only applies at the high school level, but what we need to do is remember that we are working with *young adults*. They must be treated as such. I personally believe that you don't learn anything about basic survival skills in the tenth grade that you haven't already learned in the ninth, and the eighth, and the seventh, etc. If a student is not willing to conform to the attendance, behavioral, and academic standards that are expected (no, required) in high school, it is time for him to do something else with his life. Federal and state monies are doled out to school districts according to the number of students in the system, so we fret and fret about our dropout rate, and we bend over backward to keep kids in school who have no interest or desire to be there, and who, quite honestly, drag everyone else down. (Ask any teacher if one disruptive student is capable of destroying an entire learning environment.) Yeah, yeah, I know— if we tightened our standards we'd see an immediate increase in unemployment, juvenile delinquency, gang activity, and all the other ills that plague our troubled society. Perhaps the best approach to solving many of those problems lies with an education system where effort and achievement are rewarded, and opportunity is earned.

Jobs I have decided that, as long as my bank account will allow it, I am going to encourage my own children not to have jobs while they are going to school. (College is another matter.) I recognize that might put them at a social disadvantage, and it will certainly place greater demands upon my wallet. Still, I'll tell them they're going to be working for the rest of their lives, and they should try other things while they can. Because everyday I see in my classroom the disadvantages of having a job—in the heads that droop toward the desk as the class wears on because they had to close at Wendy's the night before; in the weary, resigned eyes as they tell me they couldn't do the assignment because of their work schedule; in the sheepish looks I get when they admit they've quit an extracurricular activity because they just don't have time. You see, they think it feels nicer to drive your own car to school than to ride the bus or be dropped off, but I know that it is far more memorable to win a speech tournament than to push another extra value meal across a chrome countertop.

Extracurricular activities When I taught straight academics, I used to resent those extracurricular sponsors and coaches who seemed to place a stronger emphasis on participating in their group than in doing my assignments. No longer. As a tennis coach I would never encourage one of my players to skip an assignment or blow off a class so they could play in a match for me. I just think that you can do both. Most teachers will admit that the best students in their classes are, for the most part, involved in many other activities besides schoolwork. And the benefits you gain by participation in extracurricular activities—lessons you learn about acquiring self-discipline, about dealing with competition, about working as a team, about coping with stress—help to develop character traits that will serve you the rest of your lifetime, something as valuable as all the knowledge you can acquire. So I've resigned myself to being chauffeur for the next ten years as I shuttle my three children from activity to activity, while they participate to their heart's content. Seems worth it to me.

Veteran teachers My wife's Aunt Faith retired this year after teaching third grade for thirty-eight years. Unbelievable. Toby O'Connor, the vocational director at my high school, received his forty-year pin a while back. Awesome. I am in the middle of my twelfth year of teaching. I have so much respect for people like Aunt Faith and Toby O'Connor that it is difficult to express. I want to stand up and applaud whenever Faith comes into the room. Someone asked Toby once when he planned to retire. "For me to retire, three things need to happen," he said. "Dr. Vollbrecht [the assistant principal] needs to wear the same tie two days in a row. Bill Tooke [a history teacher] needs to have no opinion about something. And the special ed kids have to quit goosing each other." Mr. O'Connor is in for the duration. I have spent the better part of this book preaching about how noble and worthwhile it is to be a teacher, and I believe that. But it is also wearing. Stress is a constant companion, you are never finished, and you live with the knowledge that you could do more. Even the good years are hard, and nobody has all good years. The "lifers" are very special people. Personally, I hope to retire when my youngest gets out of high school, eight years from now. I better keep writing.

Girls playing football The court ruled on it this year. If a girl wants to play football in high school, any good ol' Texas football coach dang well better not tell her she can't. We just had a football coaches' convention here in San Antonio, and their response to the ruling was decidedly lukewarm. What I suspect we will see is a begrudging compliance. What I fear we might see (on more than one occasion) is a coach pulling aside a 260-pound lineman and telling him to knock the new "prospect" on her butt as many times as it takes. They start practicing football here in August, when 100 degrees is not uncommon. They start in helmets and pads after one week. Most coaches think that will take care of the problem. I'm not so sure. But there is another intriguing side to this. In Texas high schools, only the girls play volleyball. Their season runs the same time as football. And I know lots of high school boys who would dearly love to play competitive volleyball, including some fine football players. So, if the girls can play football, the boys could . . . Nah, it'd never work.

31
GRADUATION DAY
What should a diploma be worth?

My daughter Bethany will begin the ninth grade this coming school year. She arrives at my high school in August. One of the perks (we must look for perks) of being a school teacher is that we have far more input in determining who will educate our own children than the average parent does. With the help of my friend the registrar, I will make sure that Beth has a certain teacher for geometry, and another for calculus, and another for chemistry, and another for English II. I will also make sure she never sets foot in the classrooms of about five teachers who pass their time at my high school. (Would I want Bethany in one of my classes? Definitely.) As a concerned parent, I want to ensure that my daughter gets the best education possible. As a teacher who has worked at the same school for seven years, I have a fair idea of what classrooms she'll need to be in for that to happen.

But the larger question is: What do I have a right to expect? In four years she will be walking across a stage, picking up her diploma, and getting on with her life, God willing. Will her twelve years of public education (thirteen, counting kindergarten) enable her to do that?

Judging from what we hear in the media, the answer is no. A *Newsweek* special issue on education reported that only seven percent of 17-year-olds have the advanced science skills they need to perform well in college-level courses, and only thirty-two percent of them knew when the Civil War took place. A college in our area created a public furor when it required half of its freshmen class to take an English composition class over because they failed the standardized writing/grammar test at the end of the semester. Business leaders everywhere complain that the educational system is not preparing youth adequately for society and the workplace.

Naturally, we teachers read these things and grimace. This must be how auto manufacturers feel when there is a massive recall. Clearly, the job is not getting done right. But allocating responsibility for that is another matter.

Which brings me to one of my pet peeves, and one which comes up as consistently as the sun. The question can be worded a number of ways, but the intent is always the same. It could happen when we're studying grammar, an infrequent occurrence in my classroom. More likely, it will arise as we begin studying a literary work. With Shakespeare, it's like clockwork.

"Why do we have to study this?" a student will say. "How will this help me get a job?"

It won't. I would imagine that a familiarity with the works of William Shakespeare would affect the employment prospects of less than one percent of the students in my classroom. At best, he might be a brief topic of conversation with a colleague over lunch. Far more commonly, we will employ a phrase from the great bard without the vaguest notion of who the originator of said phrase was. There is, in fact, something rotten in Denmark.

I am a teacher—I am not a vocational trainer. Certainly, vocational training has its place in the high school. We offer a wealth of courses at our school—from agriculture to auto mechanics to microcomputers. Such courses make up a valuable part of the high school curriculum, and I personally favor expanding the vocational offerings on the high school level. Further, no subject, least of all English, should be devoid of practical value for getting ahead in the world. I tell all my students that if they can learn to express themselves well, orally and in writing, their chances for career advancement will be considerably increased, no matter what their field of endeavor. We spend more time in my class trying to improve our communication skills than we do on anything else.

What bothers me is this pervasive idea that education and job training are synonymous. That's like thinking you go to a ballpark to eat hot dogs. Imagine living your life in such a way that everything you did, every waking minute, was directly related to your job. What a sad life! There is so much more to living, and to learning, than what we do to earn money.

Limiting your concept of education to a means of securing employment has another dismal effect. Learning becomes finite. After you obtain a diploma, or a bachelor's degree, or a master's, or a doctorate, you are finished. Learned it all. I have heard some high school seniors say on the last day of school, "It's over. I'm never opening another book in my life." In some cases, I believe them.

So what do I want for Bethany when she crosses that stage four years from now? First of all, I expect her to have a firm sense of *who* and *where* she is. If she comes out of high school with that, she's already a step up on most of her peers. I don't know what it is, maybe MTV, but young people today have such a limited sense of their world. For all the talk of a global village, our high school graduates seem to suffer from "localitis." If it doesn't directly affect me, it doesn't exist.

There is a great passage in the play *Our Town* in which Rebecca tells of a strange letter. It was addressed:

Jane Crofut
The Crofut Farm
Grover's Corners
Sutton County
New Hampshire
United States of America
Continent of North America
Western Hemisphere
the Earth

the Solar System
the Universe
the Mind of God

After we read that passage, I have an extra credit assignment for my students. They have to write themselves a note expressing an idea, something they have learned to be true, something they want to remember. Then they must mail it to themselves, using the above address with appropriate changes. They get the extra credit when I see the returned, postmarked letter. And they get an expanded view of their world.

I would also like to see Beth cross the stage with a strong set of practical values. No, I'm not talking religion or morals here. But she should know for sure by the time she gets out of high school that there is a direct correlation between the effort she puts forth and what she achieves. She should know that the only kind of lasting discipline is self-discipline. She should know that the most limiting force in the world operates within her own mind, and that she's the captain of her ship. She should be ready for the world.

Most of all, she should be ready to *continue* her education. Graduation Day is not a destination; it's a passage. In my family we were all expected to go to college when we finished high school. We did, but for some of us getting through college was a circuitous journey. (Remember, I graduated from college when I was 31.) I am not going to insist that any of my children go to college. But whatever ambition they choose to pursue after high school, I'll be extremely disappointed if they don't proceed with a respect for knowledge and an eagerness to learn.

We had a mini-crisis at my school recently. A senior who failed a class and didn't earn the adequate credits still wanted to be able to cross the stage with his graduating class. His parents were quite insistent about it and even threatened the principal with legal intervention. Thank heavens, our principal did not buckle under to the pressure. If we start recognizing students for *participating* in high school for four years, a diploma has become meaningless.

Some barn swallows built a nest under the eaves of my front

porch this summer. I got a firsthand view of the family process. It started out with two birds, working industriously on the nest in the daytime and spending their nights together on a wind chime that hung from my porch ceiling. Then mama laid the eggs and sat on them until they hatched. We had five baby birds sticking their heads out of the nest and screaming like banshees whenever mom or dad flew in with another food delivery. Every time we let our cat out, the adult birds swooped at it mercilessly until it left the vicinity of the front porch. But the very coolest part of the whole process was when those little birds got up on the edge of that nest, teetered precariously, fluttered their wings endlessly, and then, under the watchful eye of their parents, flew. That was magic.

I expect my children to leave home when they graduate from high school. Maybe not immediately. With finances being what they are, one might have to commute to college while still living at home. One might choose not to attend college. One might go straight into the NBA(!). Still, in some symbolic, mystical way, walking across that stage means leaving. I'm sure my children will teeter and flutter as they make their way through high school, but when they're done I want them to be able to fly. Magic.

32

THE FIRST DAY OF SCHOOL
The more things change,
the more they stay the same

I like first days. Oh, I can't say that as the summer wears down and the next school year looms ahead I get all chirpy, but once I'm there and that first bell rings, I know I am where I belong. Not a bad feeling.

I like standing in the hallway in front of my door when that first bell rings. New students, new couples, new clothes.

The freshmen are easiest to spot. Poor fish. They look so scared, peering at the numbers over each classroom door, trying desperately to stay out of anybody's way, anxious to deposit themselves into a classroom, any classroom, and be safe. (Yes, I suppose I am idealizing a little. There is also the new breed of freshmen, anxious to do nothing but acquire a *baad* reputation as soon as possible.) But upperclassmen still enjoy misdirecting freshmen, and selling them phony maps and hall passes, and harassing them for stepping on the school seal, and all of that stuff that makes high school high school.

Summer romance remains as constant as William Shakespeare's poetry. The wise teacher makes it a point to stay very detached from the intricacies of the dating scene within a high school student body. Still, we can't help but notice, and to judge accordingly. I always groan inwardly when I see a sweet, young girl whom I taught the

132

previous year tucked under the arm of a boy of questionable morals whose primary form of exercise involves bending an elbow to raise a beer can to his lips. I feel equally mystified, but a lot happier, upon observing youngsters experiencing love for the first time. We tend to forget that not everyone comes to high school played out and jaded. The sight of two young people completely caught up in each other, oblivious to others, wholeheartedly devoted, is enough to make me wish I was young again (but not for long). Because you want it to last for them (and you know it won't).

Ah yes, new clothes. The first day of school ranks right behind the first day after Christmas vacation for *haute couture*. The natives will be *stylin'*. One of my tennis players came into our first class this year bragging that he'd spent $150 the previous day on school clothes.

"What did you get?" I asked him.

"Two shirts and a pair of pants."

(I have three children headed for high school, and I'm scared!)

I like to watch them (the dreaded *them*) come into my classroom. Some move immediately to the back of the room, seeking that point farthest away from me, as if I have herpes or halitosis, hoping (in vain) that I will allow them to keep their distance for the rest of eternity. Others sit front and center, perky as petunias, eyes bright and eager, like desperate candidates at a job interview. Most think nothing of me, eyes darting around the room scoping out who else will share their English class and seating themselves accordingly. The pretty girls never sit alone.

I like to see what they bring to class on that first day. There are always a few who travel light, having already lost their schedules and failing to produce even a pencil or piece of paper, should the teacher (outrageously) want to get right down to business. It's easy to spot the ones whose mothers still play an active role in their lives. New book bag, organized notebook, two of everything. It's fun watching how quickly they can trash their mother's best efforts. But the ones who really amaze me are those kids who manage, on that very first day, to look as if they've been attending classes the past six months. You'd think they had moved out of their homes to come back to school, their book bags loaded down with every imaginable thing. Put a brand new textbook in their hands and watch it transmogrify instantaneously. And they can do it with new desks, new clothes, new shoes . . .

I have a fairly standard set of procedures I follow on the first day, some imposed by the administration, others invented by me. Taking roll, naturally. Only three things really concern me regarding the class roster—the ratio of boys to girls, whether I have any repeaters from previous years, and if I have drawn any of the known troublemakers/juvenile delinquents that attend our school. Having a good male/female balance is always a good sign for a class. Having an overabundance of boys can be hellish. (This year I have fifteen boys and three girls in my second period class—it's getting pretty testy in there.) I resent repeaters. My class is usually fun, and it is not hard to pass if you do the work. If a student is a repeater, it means he had the fun without doing the work. I hate that. As far as the troublemakers go, there's not much I can do. On that first day, I try to let them know that I know who they are, and that I'm willing to withhold personal judgment. Some of those kids do better in my class than they do in most other classes. Many of them . . . well, you can't win them all.

Then it's time for classroom rules. I discourage eating and drinking, and they have to spit their gum out if I see them chewing (it makes their faces look ugly). I try to enforce the school's tardy policy (which is always changing and never effective). I discourage people from leaving my classroom, but I am not without compassion. I have sat trapped in a classroom with a bladder or bowel about to explode, and I wouldn't wish that on anyone. If nature calls, we must respond. If nature calls frequently, see a doctor.

On to the seating chart. I do that the same way every year. They all put their names in a hat, and I select a Vanna White to draw. As she picks names, I give a little speech about fate and destiny, how who you sit next to in English II class could end up being one of the most significant events of your life, certainly not something to be controlled by a mere teacher, but rather something to be left up to whatever Higher Power you choose to believe in. I get downright flowery about it. (Incidentally, if the chart doesn't work out, I don't hesitate to change it.)

I end that first day of class trying to find out about the people I will be teaching. I use a personal information card, which contains relevant information (home and work phone numbers, extracurricular activities) and irrelevant information (their all-time favorite movie, what they expect to be doing in ten years). What I ask about them, I tell about myself.

It all boils down to making a first impression. I want them to look forward to my class. I want them to feel it is a place to be active, not passive. No doubt that's a dangerous approach. Unleashing youthful energy is an invitation to chaos. But if I can get them sitting in second period thinking, Oh good, I have English next . . . if I can have them enter my classroom with a positive attitude about being there . . . if I can cajole them to think about what we are doing —then, I have a step up on most. And a teacher always looks for an edge.

I like lots of other things about the first day of school. I like seeing the new members of the faculty, mentally gauging to myself whether they are cut out for this line of work or not. I like seeing which teachers share my conference period. Who is in the faculty lounge at that time will determine how much of my conference period I spend down there, and how much I spend in my room, and, consequently, how much I will accomplish during that period. (Any teacher with sense avoids the faculty lounge like the plague! There is a good reason it's called a lounge.) I like teasing fifth-year seniors if I am friendly with them. I like getting mail out of my teacher mailbox again. I like tennis practice.

But what I like most is the progression. Every year starts with a first day, and every year ends with a last day. The alpha and the omega. The first day is fun. The last day, ah, that's another thing entirely. On the last day, we enter celestial realms.

DALLIN MALMGREN is a high school English teacher and tennis coach in a school district near San Antonio that reflects all the problems and possibilities of our educational system. He is also the author of several novels for young readers.